TALK

Italian

1

ALWENA LAMPING

Author and Series Editor

BBC Active, an imprint of Educational Publishers LLP, part of the Pearson Education Group, Edinburgh Gate, Harlow, Essex CM20 2JE, England

First published 1998
Third edition 2014
9

ISBN 978-1-406-67894-9

Editor: Sarah Boas
Development editor: Liviana Ferrari
Additional editing: Tara Alner
Project editor: Emma Brown
Insides design: Nicolle Thomas, Rob Lian
Layout: Pantek Media Ltd. www.pantekmedia.co.uk
Illustrations © Mark Duffin
Cover design: Two Associates
Cover photograph: © iStock.com/mrdoomits
Audio producer: John Green, TEFL tapes
Sound engineer: Tim Woolf
Presenters: Aldo Alessio, Jessica Juffré, Massimo Marinoni, Anna-Maria Rubino
Studio: Robert Nichol Audio Productions
Music: Peter Hutchings

www.bbcactivelanguages.com

Printed and bound in China (CTPSC/09)

The Publisher's policy is to use paper manufactured from sustainable forests.

Pearson Education is not responsible for the content of third-party websites.

Contents

Introduction

Welcome to the new edition of **Talk Italian**, the bestselling course from BBC Active which has inspired and helped so many people to learn Italian from scratch and given them the confidence to have a go.

The key to **Talk Italian**'s effectiveness is the successful **Talk** method, developed by experienced teachers of languages to adult beginners. Its structured and systematic approach encourages you to make genuine progress and promotes a real sense of achievement. The choice of situations and vocabulary is based on the everyday needs of people travelling to Italy.

Talk Italian includes a book and 120 minutes of recordings of Italian native speakers. The book in this new edition has several additional features, inspired by feedback from users and teachers. There's an extended grammar section (pages 119–130), a two-way glossary (pages 131–144), covering around 1,000 words, and the ever-popular **Talk** *Wordpower* (pages 127–129), designed to increase your vocabulary fast.

There are also links to the **Talk Italian** video clips and activities on the BBC Languages website at www.bbcactivelanguages.com/ItalianVideoLinks. These cover the contents of this book at the same level but in an alternative way, providing additional exposure and reinforcing the language against the background of Italian culture. Free tutors' support and activities are available online at www.bbcactivelanguages.com.

How to make the most of Talk Italian

1   Read the first page of the unit to focus on what you're aiming to learn and set it in context while gaining some relevant vocabulary.

2   Listen to the key phrases – don't be tempted to read them first. Then listen to them again, this time reading them in your book too. Finally, try reading them out loud before listening one more time.

3   Work your way through the activities which follow the key phrases. These highlight key language elements and are carefully designed to develop your listening skills and your understanding of Italian. You can check your answers at any time in the *Transcripts and answers* starting on page 101.

> Wherever you see this: **1•5**, the phrases or dialogues are recorded on the CD (i.e. CD1, track 5).

4   Read the *In italiano* explanations of how Italian works as you come to them – this information is placed just where you need it. And if you'd like to know more, visit the relevant pages in the *Grammar* section, indicated by the following symbol: **G13** . For an even deeper level of knowledge, there's a separate **Talk Italian Grammar** book.

5   After completing the activities, and before you try the *Put it all together* section, close your book and listen to the conversations straight through. The more times you listen, the more familiar Italian will become and the more comfortable you'll become with it. You might also like to read the dialogues at this stage (page 101) – preferably out loud.

6   Complete the consolidation activities in *Put it all together* and check your answers with the *Transcripts and answers*.

7   Use the Italian you have learnt – the native speaker presenters on the audio will prompt you and guide you through the *Now you're talking!* section as you practise speaking Italian.

8   Check your progress. First, test your knowledge with the *Quiz*. Then assess whether you can do everything on the checklist – if in doubt, go back and spend some more time on the relevant section.

9   Read the learning hint at the end of the unit, which provides ideas and suggestions on how to use your study time effectively or how to extend your knowledge. Watch the video clip and follow any links that interest you.

10 Finally, relax and listen to the whole unit, understanding what the people are saying in Italian and taking part in the conversations.

When you've completed the course, go and use your Italian and enjoy the sense of achievement. If you want to carry on learning, **Talk Italian 2** is there waiting for you, as is the **Talk Italian Grammar**, which is so much more than an ordinary grammar book.

Pronunciation guide

The best way to acquire a good Italian accent is to listen to the audio often and to imitate the speakers closely.

1   Italian **vowels** are consistent and pure sounds.

a	ha		*cat*
a	pane		*cart*
e/è	sette		*get*
e/é	sera		*ace*
i	vino	*as in …*	*meet*
o	notte		*pot*
o	come		*pour*
u	due		*cool*

2   Most **consonants** are similar in Italian and English but the following need attention:

c	+ **e** or **i**	cena, ciao	church
	+ all other letters	come, caro	cot
ch		che, chilo	kilo
g	+ **e** or **i**	gelato, giorno	jeans
	+ **n**	signore	canyon
	+ **li**	famiglia	million
	+ other letters	guida	get
h	always silent	ha	
r	trilled as Scottish r	sera	rose
s		sono	soup
	between two vowels	francese	rise
	+ **ce** or **ci**	pesce	ship
	+ **c** + other letters	scontrino	school
z	has two sounds	zucchero	pads
		pizza	pits

Double consonants are pronounced very emphatically and the sound is prolonged.

3   As a general rule, Italian words are stressed on the last syllable but one, but there are many exceptions which can best be learned gradually by listening. Some words have a written accent to indicate the stress: **città**, **caffè**.

Buongiorno!

saying hello and goodbye

introducing yourself

... and getting to know people

In Italia ... *In Italy ...*

greetings tend to be less casual than in many English-speaking countries. When greeting someone and saying goodbye, you often add their name. If you are talking to someone whose name you don't know, you address a man as **signore** and a woman as **signora**. When followed by a surname, **signore** loses its final **-e** to become **signor**.

Saying hello

1 **1•02** Listen to these key phrases.

Buongiorno.	Hello, good morning.
Buona sera.	Hello, good afternoon/evening.
Ciao.	Hi.
Come sta?	How are you?
Bene, grazie ...	Fine, thank you ...
... e lei?	... and you?

2 **1•03** It's 9 a.m. Listen as Maria Cavalleri, the receptionist at the Albergo Giotto, greets people at reception.

> **Buongiorno, signore**

Is the first person she talks to a man or a woman?

She addresses two people by name.
Listen and put **signor** or **signora** next to their names.

.... **Chiesa**
.... **Riccardi**

3 **1•04** From mid-afternoon through into the evening, she uses a different greeting. Having heard the key phrases, what greeting would you expect her to use?

4 **1•05** Listen as Carla, Giorgio and some other friends greet each other in the foyer. How many times do you hear **ciao** and **buongiorno**?

In italiano ... *In Italian ...*

you can use **ciao** (or **buongiorno**) to greet someone you know well. To ask how he or she is, you say **Come stai?**

... and goodbye

5 **1•06** Listen to these key phrases.

Arrivederci.	Goodbye.
Buona notte.	Goodnight, goodbye.
Ciao.	Bye.

6 **1•07** Signor Conti is saying goodbye as he leaves the hotel. Listen out for **buongiorno** which is often used when saying goodbye, to wish someone a nice day. Later in the day **buona sera** can be used in the same way.

7 **1•08** Angela and Francesca leave next. Listen to the conversation then fill the gaps.

Francesca   .... **Angela** ....
Angela   .... **Francesca** ....

8 **1•09** It is now late evening and more guests are leaving.
How many are men and how many are women?

> Buona notte, signora

9 How would you greet the following people at the times indicated?

9.30 a.m.	signor Calvi, a business acquaintance
5.00 p.m.	Carlo, a good friend
5.00 p.m.	the man giving information in the tourist office
10.00 p.m.	Maria Cavalleri, the hotel receptionist
8.00 a.m.	Lucia, a friend's daughter, who's 12

10 Now try the following. How would you:

- ask signor Calvi how he is?
- ask Carlo how he is?
- say goodbye to signor Calvi?

Introducing yourself

1   **1•10** Listen to these key phrases.

Io sono ...   I'm ...
Lei è ...   You are ...

The words **io** *I* and **lei** *you* are often omitted.

2   **1•11** The receptionist has a problem
identifying some of the guests arriving
at a conference in the hotel. Listen and
decide if she has written down the right
names. Correct any that are wrong.

Giovanna Ricci

Paolo Riccardi

Enrico Piacenza

3   **1•12** The next person walks past without checking in. Listen as the
receptionist asks him who he is and focus on the words she uses.

Maria   **Buongiorno, signore. Signore, lei è ...?**
signor Mancini   **Mancini. Sono Luciano Mancini.**

4   **1•13** Listen to these key phrases.

Come si chiama?   What's your name?
Mi chiamo ...   My name is ...
Piacere.   Pleased to meet you.
Scusi?   Excuse me?

5   **1•14** Listen as Luciano Mancini and Francesca Como meet each other
for the first time. Tick the key phrases in activity 4 as you hear them.

6   **1•15** Enrico Piacenza doesn't quite catch Giovanna Ricci's name.
How does he ask her to repeat it?

... and getting to know people

7   **1•16** Outside the hotel, Mario is also getting to know people. The question he asks younger people is **Come ti chiami?** Listen to the dialogue then fill the gaps.

Mario	**Buongiorno. Come si .... ?**
sig. Lelli	**........ chiamo Franco Lelli.**
Mario	**Ciao. .... ti chiami?**
Giulia	**........ chiamo Giulia.**
Mario	**E tu, come ti chiami?**
Marcella	**Mi .... Marcella.**

In italiano ...

lei and **tu** both mean *you*. You use

> **lei** to someone you don't know well or someone older than yourself;
> **tu** to a friend, member of the family or a young person.

The choice affects other words:

lei	**Come si chiama?**	**Come sta?**
tu	**Come ti chiami?**	**Come stai?**

If in doubt use **lei**, especially to an older person.   **G6**

---

8   **1•17** Tick any of the following names that you hear in this conversation in the hotel bar.

Gianna	**Gemma**	**Gregorio**	**Giorgio**
Guido	**Giovanna**	**Geraldo**	**Giulia**

Choose three of the names and work out how these people would introduce themselves.

Have you noticed that many women's names in Italian end in **-a** while men's names tend to end in **-o**?

put it all together

1 Match the English with the Italian.

a	Goodnight.	Buona sera.
b	Hi.	Arrivederci.
c	My name's …	Come si chiama?
d	I am …	Ciao.
e	Good morning.	Piacere.
f	How are you?	Buongiorno.
g	Goodbye.	Mi chiamo …
h	Good evening.	Buona notte.
i	What's your name?	Io sono …
j	Pleased to meet you.	Come sta?

2 What could these people be saying to each other?

a

b

c

d

3 The following names are all in this unit. Try saying them out loud, then listen again to the conversations to check your pronunciation. **C** before **e** and **i** sounds like **ch** in *church*, but it has a hard **k** sound before all other letters.

Maria Cavalleri	signor Riccardi	signor Conti
Carla	Giorgio	Franco
signor Chiesa	Francesca	Enrico Piacenza
Giovanna Ricci	Luciano Mancini	Marcella

now you're talking!

1   **1•18** Imagine it's lunchtime and you're in the hotel bar at the Albergo Giotto. A man standing by the bar greets you.

- **Buongiorno. Come sta?**
- ◆ Say you're fine; ask how he is.
- **Bene, grazie.**

A woman comes in and joins you.

- ◆ Greet her and introduce yourself.
- **Piacere. Io sono Anna Alberti.**
- ◆ You didn't catch her name. Say *Excuse me?*
- **Anna Alberti.**
- ◆ Say you're pleased to meet her.

Someone else arrives – you think his name is Luciano Mironi but you're not sure.

- ◆ Greet him and ask him if he is Luciano Mironi.
- **No, sono Luciano Mancini.**
- ◆ Say who you are and that you're pleased to meet him.
- **Piacere.**

You have to leave.

- ◆ Say goodbye to Anna and Luciano.
- **Arrivederci.**

2   **1•19** Later, at around 6 p.m., you're in reception.

- ◆ Greet the receptionist.
- **Buona sera. Come sta?**
- ◆ Say you're fine, then say hello to her daughter.
- **Buona sera.**
- ◆ Ask her what her name is.
- **Mi chiamo Giulia.**
- ◆ Ask Giulia how she is.
- **Bene, grazie.**
- ◆ Say goodbye and wish them a nice evening.

quiz

1 When would you use **Ciao**?
2 What's the Italian for *Pleased to meet you*?
3 When do you use **Buona sera**?
4 Would you use **tu** or **lei** when speaking to someone you don't know very well?
5 When does **signore** shorten to **signor**?
6 How would you reply if someone asked you **Come sta**?
7 When do you say **Buona notte**?
8 What are the two ways of introducing yourself?
9 In which one of these three names does the letter **c** have a hard **k** sound: **Gucci   Versace   Moschino**?
10 When asking a child's name, would you ask **Come si chiama?** or **Come ti chiami?**

Now check whether you can ...

- greet someone correctly during the day – morning, afternoon and evening
- say goodnight and say goodbye
- introduce yourself
- reply when someone is introduced to you
- ask someone's name and give your name
- ask someone how they are
- reply when someone asks you how you are
- ask for clarification if you didn't catch what was said

Listen to the audio as often as you can and try to imitate the people on it as closely as possible. Listening to things over and over again and repeating them many times will help you get familiar with the sounds of Italian. When you practise, say the words and phrases out loud.

Di dov'è?

talking about where you're from

... and your nationality

saying what you do for a living

giving your phone number

In Italia ...

people tend to be friendly and open, and it is well worth learning to say a little about yourself and to ask simple questions, so that you can make conversation with the Italians you meet.

You'll find many Italians will refer to the town or the region they come from and say that they are, for example, **fiorentino** (from **Firenze** *Florence*), **romano** (from **Roma**), **bolognese** (from **Bologna**), or **siciliano** (from **Sicilia**).

Talking about where you're from

1 **1•20** Listen to these key phrases.

(Lei) è inglese?	Are you English? (formal)
(Tu) sei inglese?	Are you English? (informal)
Sì – sono inglese.	Yes – I'm English.
No – non sono inglese.	No – I'm not English.
Di dov'è?	Where are you from? **(lei)**
Di dove sei?	Where are you from? **(tu)**
Sono di ...	I'm from ...

2 **1•21** Fiorella, a student doing some market research for an Italian holiday company, talks to a group of English-speaking visitors in Verona. Tick their nationalities as you hear them.

	inglese	australiano/a	americano/a
signora 1			
signore 1			
signore 2			
signora 2			

> **In italiano ...**
>
> there are two types of adjectives (words which describe things, e.g. *big*, *Italian*, *married*, *green*, *this*, *my*):
> - ending in **-e**: **inglese**
> - ending in **-o**: **americano** (the **-o** changes to **-a** when describing females: **americana**)
>
> G4

3 **1•22** Listen as one of the other students now asks Fiorella about herself. Does he ask **Di dov'è?** or **Di dove sei?**

Which of these northern Italian towns is she from?

Brescia   **Bergamo**   **Bolzano**

... and your nationality

4 Can you match these nationalities to the countries? Two have been done for you.

italiano   francese   spagnolo   svizzero   tedesco   australiano
scozzese   gallese   inglese   irlandese   canadese   americano

Paese		Nazionalità
Italia	*Italy*	....
Inghilterra	*England*	....
Scozia	*Scotland*	....
Irlanda	*Ireland*	....
Galles	*Wales*	....
Stati Uniti	*USA*	*americano*
Australia	*Australia*	....
Svizzera	*Switzerland*	....
Francia	*France*	....
Germania	*Germany*	*tedesco*
Spagna	*Spain*	....
Canada	*Canada*	....

Now tick the nationalities which change when describing a woman.

5 **1•23** Listen to the way some of these countries and nationalities are pronounced and repeat them, taking care to imitate the clear sounds of the vowels – **a e i o u**.

In italiano ...

è means *is, he is, she is* and *it is* as well as *you are*.   **G9**

---

6 **1•24** Fiorella tells a colleague about some of the people she interviewed. Listen to the conversation then fill the gaps.

Antonio è .... **, di Madrid.**
Helen è ....
Mike è di Toronto, è ....
Anna è .... **È di Edimburgo.**

Saying what you do for a living

1 **1•25** Listen to these key phrases.

Che lavoro fa?	What do you do? **(lei)**
Che lavoro fai?	What do you do? **(tu)**
Sono infermiera.	I'm a nurse.
Sono in pensione.	I'm retired.
Non sono studente.	I'm not a student.

2 **1•26** Listen as Fiorella asks three people what they do for a living. Work out which one is an engineer, which one a journalist and which one a secretary.

signore ....

signora 1 ....

signora 2 ....

ingegnere
giornalista
segretaria

In italiano ...

the words *a/an* are not used when saying what you do:

Sono casalinga.	*I'm a housewife.*
Sono architetto.	*I'm an architect.*

G3

---

3 **1•27** Fiorella continues with her survey. Listen, then fill the gaps with words from the list on the right. What do you think the word **ma** means?

Notice that some occupations have a masculine and a feminine form.

Fiorella	**Che lavoro fa?**
	Sono ....
Fiorella	**Tu sei studente?**
	No, non sono studente.
Fiorella	**Che lavoro fai?**
	Sono ....
Fiorella	**Lei è artista?**
	Sì, ma sono ....

professore/essa *teacher*
ragioniere/a *accountant*
impiegato/a *office worker*
direttore *manager*
guida *tour guide*
medico *doctor*
disoccupato/a *unemployed*

4   **1•28** Fiorella asks another man about his occupation and his nationality. Listen, then make a note of his answers in Italian and English.

lavoro: ....……...

nazionalità: ....……...

Giving your phone number

1   **1•29** Look at the following numbers 0 to 10 and then listen to them on the audio.

0   1   2   3   4   5   6   7   8   9   10
zero uno due tre quattro cinque sei sette otto nove dieci

2   **1•30** Two people give Fiorella their **numero di telefono** *phone number*. Listen, then make a note of them.

Gemma   ....…….......

Paolo   ....…….......

3   Say these two phone numbers out loud.

01604 299 385
00 39 51 561 486

Now practise saying your own **numero di telefono**, at home and at work, your mobile number, and the numbers of friends and family.

put it all together

1 Which answer best fits each question?

a	Signora, lei è inglese?	Sono infermiera.
b	Lei è italiano, signore?	No, io sono romano.
c	Di dov'è?	No, sono americana.
d	Lei è di Firenze?	No, non sono italiano.
e	Che lavoro fa?	Sono di Milano.

2 Marco Manuzzi is an Italian doctor from Florence.
How would he fill in this form? (**Cognome** means *surname*).

Cognome .... Nome ....
Nazionalità ....
Professione ....

3 Fill the gaps in the sentence about Ulrike with:

tedesca   chiamo   dentista

**Mi .... Ulrike Schmitt. Sono ....,
di Berlino e sono ....**

Using the above as your guide,
work out what Angela and Marco
would say about
themselves.

> Marco Blondini
> accountant
> Italian, from Rome

> Angela Roberts
> secretary
> Welsh, from Bangor

4 The following places and professions have all been used in
this unit. How are they pronounced?

Galles Germania Edimburgo giornalista guida ingegnere

g + e or i sounds like **j** in *jeans*, **gn** sounds like **ny** in *canyon*
gl sounds like **lli** in *million*, g + anything else sounds like **g** in *go*

now you're talking!

1   **1•31** You are on holiday in Verona and someone asks you where the town hall is. When you tell them you are not from here – **non sono di qui** – it leads to a conversation. You need to know how to:

- ◆ say you're not from here
- ◆ say you're English, from Chester
- ◆ find out where he's from

2   **1•32** Now imagine you are Andrew Fairlie and play his part in the conversation.

Name: Andrew Fairlie
Occupation: Architect
Nationality: Scottish
Home Town: Edinburgh

- ● **Signor Fairlie, lei è inglese?**
- ● **Di dov'è?**
- ● **Che lavoro fa?**

3   **1•33** Still in Verona, you start chatting to someone in your hotel. Listen to the questions and this time answer them with information about yourself.

- ● **Buongiorno! Come sta?**
- ● **Sono Pietro. Lei, come si chiama?**
- ● **Lei è americano?**
- ● **Di dov'è?**
- ● **Che lavoro fa?**

quiz

1 Would an Italian woman say **Sono italiano** or **Sono italiana**?

2 How would you tell someone you're from Chester?

3 What are the missing numbers in the sequence?

   due, ..., sei, ..., dieci

4 In a formal working situation, how would you ask someone where they're from?

5 What changes would you make to your answer to question 4 if you were chatting to a young student?

6 How do you say *I'm not from here* in Italian?

7 Which of the following is the odd one out?

   impiegato canadese tedesco francese

8 If a woman tells you she is **fiorentina**, where is she from?

9 What word would you have to add for this sentence to mean *I'm not a housewife?* .... **sono casalinga**.

10 If **attrice** is a female **attore** *actor*, what's the Italian for a female **autore** *author?*

Now check whether you can ...

- say where you're from
- say what nationality you are
- say what you do for a living
- ask others for the above information
- use the numbers 0 to 10
- give your phone number

When learning new words and phrases, write them out. Whether it's on paper, your phone, a computer or tablet, the actual process of reproducing them helps to fix them in your memory.

Make your vocabulary bank relevant to you and your lifestyle – it's much easier to remember words that are important to you.

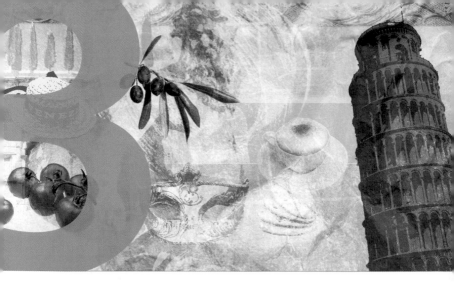

Questo è Paolo

introducing friends and colleagues

... and family

saying how old you are

talking about your family

In Italia ...

the tendency is towards smaller families than in the past, but **la famiglia** *the family* is still the focal point in the lives of most Italians. Don't be surprised to be asked questions about yourself and your family and don't be reserved about asking questions.

The Italians' affection for **bambini** *children* is legendary and they are welcome almost everywhere. You won't have to request special treatment in restaurants since children regularly eat out with their parents, even late into the evening.

Introducing friends and colleagues

1   **1•34** Listen to these key phrases.

     Questo è ...   This is ... (to introduce a man)
     e   and
     Questa è ...   This is ... (to introduce a woman)

2   **1•35** Mario Grada, who knows many of the conference delegates in the hotel, makes some introductions. Listen to the conversation then fill the gaps.

Mario	**Buongiorno, signora Cesare.**
	.... **è Paolo Lega.**
sig. Lega	**Piacere.**
Mario	**E ....** **è Camilla Faldi.**
sig.ra Cesare	**Piacere.**

> **Piacere**

3   **1•36** Listen to these key phrases.

     Questo è mio marito.   This is my husband.
     Questa è mia moglie.   This is my wife.
     Sono sposato/a.   I'm married.
     ... divorziato/a.   ... divorced.

4   **1•37** Over an informal lunch, Camilla and Paolo introduce their partners to Mario. Listen and tick the right names.

Camilla's husband is   ☐ **Piero**   ☐ **Pietro**
Paolo's wife is   ☐ **Maria**   ☐ **Marta**

5   **1•38** Some more people join them. Note that they use the informal **tu**. Listen and work out who is married and who isn't.

	Mario	Alessandra	Ettore
sposato/a			
divorziato/a			
single			

... and family

6 **1•39** Listen to these key phrases.

Ha figli?/Ha bambini?	Do you have children?
Ho ...	I have ...
... un figlio.	... a son.
... una figlia.	... a daughter.
Non ho figli.	I don't have children.

In italiano ...

uno *one* changes to **un** before a male and **una** before a female;
una is shortened to **un'** before a vowel: **un'amica** *a friend*;
un, uno, una and **un'** are also the words for *a/an*.   **G3**

---

7 **1•40** **Figli** (literally *sons*) and **bambini** are both used for *children* –
bambini usually for younger children. Listen to Camilla and Marta
talking about their children. Do they have sons or daughters?

Mario	**Hai bambini, Camilla?**
Camilla	**Sì, ho** .... **e** ....
Mario	**E tu, Marta, hai bambini?**
Marta	**Ho** .... **Roberto! Questo è** ....

8 **1•41** Mario then talks to Renata.
Is she married?
Does she have children?

ho	*I have*
hai	*you have* (**tu**)
ha	*you have* (**lei**)

9 How would you introduce the following?

- Enrico Piacenza
- Francesca
- your partner

Saying how old you are

1 **1•42** Listen to some of the following numbers.

11	**undici**	21	**ventuno**	40	**quaranta**
12	**dodici**	22	**ventidue**	50	**cinquanta**
13	**tredici**	23	**ventitré**	60	**sessanta**
14	**quattordici**	24	**ventiquattro**	70	**settanta**
15	**quindici**	25	**venticinque**	80	**ottanta**
16	**sedici**	26	**ventisei**	90	**novanta**
17	**diciassette**	27	**ventisette**	100	**cento**
18	**diciotto**	28	**ventotto**		
19	**diciannove**	29	**ventinove**		
20	**venti**	30	**trenta**		

31–99 follow the same pattern as 21–29: **trentuno, trentadue, trentatré**, etc.

2 **1•43** You will hear all but one of the following numbers. Which one is it?
14   100   54   29   36

3 Say the following numbers out loud.
15   55   12   46   87   73

4 **1•44** Listen to these key phrases.

Quanti anni ha?	How old are you? **(lei)**
Quanti anni hai?	How old are you? **(tu)**
Ho 19 anni.	I'm 19.

5 **1•45** Out by the hotel pool, Mario listens to some students chatting. Listen and note down their ages. **Anch'io** means *me too*.

Massimo   ....
Laura   ....
Marianna   ....

... and talking about your family

6 **1•46** Mario listens to two women talking about their families. Listen to the conversation then fill the gaps.

signora 1	**Lei ha figli?**
signora 2	**Ho una ...., Caterina, e ho anche un ....**
signora 1	**Come si ....?**
signora 2	**Stefano.**
signora 1	**Quanti anni ....?**
signora 2	**Ha .... anni.**

7 **1•47** Listen to Anna, Alessandra and Lorenzo introducing their families and decide which family belongs to whom. (**padre** *father*, **sorella** *sister*)

a ....   b ....   c ....

put it all together

1 Questa è la famiglia Archenti.

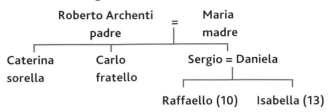

Roberto Archenti _ Maria
padre = madre

Caterina   Carlo   Sergio = Daniela
sorella   fratello

Raffaello (10)   Isabella (13)

Look at Sergio Archenti's family tree and choose the correct ending for his statements.

a **Mio padre si chiama**   Raffaello   Roberto
b **Mia sorella si chiama**   Daniela   Caterina
c **Isabella è**   mia madre   mia figlia
d **Isabella ha**   sedici anni   tredici anni

Are the following **vero** *true* or **falso** *false*?

	vero	falso
e **Daniela è sposata.**		
f **Sergio ha un fratello e un figlio.**		
g **Il fratello di Isabella si chiama Carlo.**		

2 Now read what Sergio says about some of his family:

Mia sorella ha quarantadue anni, anche mio fratello Carlo – sono gemelli.

Can you work out what **gemelli** are?

3 **Ha fratelli?** is the way to ask someone if they have any brothers and sisters. Would you answer **Sì** or **No** if you were asked **Ha fratelli?** and **Ha figli?** If the answer is **Sì**, can you provide more details, giving their names and ages?

now you're talking!

1　**1•48** Read these questions and then be guided by the audio. Answer as if you were Anna Fraser, married to Jonathan, with two children, Sarah (14) and Daniel (12).

Suo and **sua** mean *your* in this conversation.

- **Buongiorno, signora. Come si chiama?**
- **Lei è sposata?**
- **Ha figli?**
- **Come si chiama sua figlia?**
- **Quanti anni ha?**
- **E suo figlio – come si chiama?**
- **Quanti anni ha?**

2　**1•49** Now, using the informal **tu**, take part in a conversation with Marco. You need to know how to:

- say whether you're married or otherwise
- ask if he is married
- ask if he has children
- ask what his daughter's name is
- ask how old she is
- introduce a friend/partner to him

quiz

1 Do you need **questo è** or **questa è** to introduce a woman?
2 How would you introduce your brother to Anna?
3 Which of the following means *my daughter*?
   mio figlio   mia figlia   sua figlia
4 What is the Italian for *sister*?
5 Does **mio padre** mean *my mother* or *my father*?
6 To ask a small child how old s/he is, would you say **Quanti anni hai?** or **Quanti anni ha?**
7 Can you say how old you are in Italian?
8 If a person **ha quindici anni**, are they 5, 15 or 50?
9 What do **quindici, sei** and **settantotto** add up to?

Now check whether you can ...

- say whether you are married or otherwise
- say what family you have
- give your age
- ask others for the above information
- introduce someone – male or female
- ask or say how old someone else is
- use the numbers 11 to 100

A good way to practise introducing people is to find a family photograph with lots of people in it – a wedding group is ideal. Pointing to each person, say who they are:

e.g. **Questa è mia madre.   Questo è mio fratello David.**

The following words might come in useful:

nonno, nonna	*grandfather, grandmother*
cugino, cugina	*cousin – male/female*
zio, zia	*uncle, aunt*

Un caffè, per favore

ordering a drink in a bar

offering someone a drink

... and accepting or refusing

In Italia ...

you're never very far from a **caffè** or **bar** – they're an important feature of the Italian lifestyle. Open from early morning until late at night, they serve snacks and a wide variety of drinks, hot and cold, alcoholic and soft.

In many bars, you pay at the **cassa** *cash desk*, then repeat your order at the bar, handing your **scontrino** *receipt* to the **barista** *barman*. It is usual to leave some loose change in the saucer on the bar.

You pay more for drinks brought to you at a table by the waiter than for drinks bought and drunk standing at the bar. The difference in price can be considerable in prime tourist areas.

Ordering a drink

1   **1•50** Listen to these key phrases.

Prego?/Mi dica.	Can I help you?
Un caffè, per favore.	A coffee, please.
Una birra, per favore.	A beer, please.
... anche per me.	... for me too.
Grazie.	Thank you.
Prego.	You're welcome.
Va bene.	OK, that's fine.

2   **1•51** Mario orders a beer while waiting in the Bar Roma for some colleagues. Listen out for the strong **r** sound in **birra**.

3   **1•52** Listen to the family next to him ordering four different drinks. Can you decide who has what?

	un caffè *black coffee*	**un gelato** *ice cream*	**una coca** *coke*	**un'aranciata** *fizzy orange*
padre				
madre				
figlio				
figlia				

In italiano ...

all nouns, not just those referring to people, are either masculine (m) or feminine (f).

Nouns ending in **-o** are nearly all masculine.
    un figlio, un cappuccino

Nouns ending in **-a** are usually feminine.
    una figlia, una birra, un'aranciata

Some nouns ending in **-e** are masculine, others are feminine.
    un padre, un bicchiere (m)
    una moglie, una notte (f)

G1

... in a bar

4 **1•53** Listen as other people arrive and order drinks.
What does the man order? ....
How does the woman say she'll have the same? ....
Does the woman have her coffee **con o senza zucchero**
with or without sugar? Or with **dolcificante** *sweetener?*

5 **1•54** Now listen to a woman ordering drinks for herself and her
daughter.
Is the mineral water she orders sparkling (**gassata**) or still (**non
gassata**)?
What does her daughter have?

Signora	**Buona sera.**
Cameriere	**Signora, buona sera. Mi dica.**
Signora	**Un'acqua minerale, per favore.**
Cameriere	**Gassata o non gassata?**
Signora	**...................... E un .... per mia figlia.**
Cameriere	**Allora, un .... e un'acqua minerale .... Va bene.**

6 **1•55** Anna and Adriano are ordering drinks. Are the following
statements **vero o falso** *true or false?*

	vero	falso
a Anna orders black coffee.		
b She takes sugar in coffee.		
c Adriano orders mineral water.		
d He prefers still water.		

7 How would you ask for:

- a beer?
- a coffee?
- an ice cream?

Offering someone a drink

1   1•57 Listen to these key phrases.

Che cosa prende?	What will you have?
Prende un caffè?	Will you have a coffee?
Per lei?/Per te?	For you?
Volentieri.	I'd love to./I'd love one.
Sì, grazie.	Yes please.
No, grazie.	No thank you.
Cin cin!	Cheers!

2   1•58 Listen as Mario's colleagues arrive and he offers them coffee.
How does signor Guarino
accept? ....
What kind of coffee does Luisa
want? ....
(You may need to consult the **In
Italia ...** box.)

In Italia ...

If you ask for **un caffè**, you'll get a small **espresso**. If you want
white coffee, order **caffellatte**, not **latte** which is just milk.
Alternatives include:
cappuccino, possibly dusted with chocolate or **cannella**
cinnamon
caffè americano, which is **caffè** in a larger cup with water added
caffè macchiato, espresso with just a trace of milk
caffè corretto, **espresso** with a shot of grappa or brandy

---

3   1•59 At the **cassa**, Franca buys a drink for Claudia and Fabio. She
uses **prendi** – the **tu** form of **prende**.

What do they all order? ....
Listen out particularly for the difference in pronunciation between
birra and **birre**.

... and accepting or refusing

In italiano ...

nouns do not add -s to form the plural. Instead, the final vowel changes:

-o and -e change to -i

un cappuccino	tre cappuccini
un bicchiere	due bicchieri
una notte	quattro notti

-a changes to -e

una birra	due birre

other letters do not change

un caffè	tre caffè
un bar	due bar

G1

---

4 **1•60** Three people order wine by the glass (**bicchiere**). Work out whether they order **vino rosso** *red wine* or **vino bianco** *white wine*.

	vino rosso	vino bianco
Antonio		
Anita		
signora Perrone		

5 **1•61** Later, Mario is with signor Guarino and an English colleague. Listen out for **Come si dice in italiano 'whisky'?** *How do you say 'whisky' in Italian?*. Do they have their whisky with or without ice (**ghiaccio**)?

	con ghiaccio	senza ghiaccio
signor Howard		
signor Guarino		

What does Mario drink?

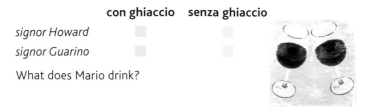

put it all together

1   Choose **un**, **una**, **un'** for each item.

.... **caffè**   .... **cappuccino**
.... **tè**   .... **acqua minerale**
.... **vino**   .... **spremuta**
.... **birra**   .... **grappa**
.... **gelato**   .... **frullato**
.... **aranciata** .... **amaro**

Check the meaning of any new words in the glossary.

2   Rearrange these sentences to form a dialogue.

E tu, Fabrizio – prendi un bicchiere di vino?
Allora due caffè e un bicchiere di vino bianco per me.
Volentieri – senza zucchero, per favore.
No grazie – un caffè anche per me.
Buongiorno, Antonia – prende un caffè?

3   The waiter is having difficulty with the orders.
Correct him as in the example, remembering
to change the endings of the words as necessary.

Cameriere	**Un gelato e due caffè?**	*Mi dica*
You	**No, due gelati e un caffè.**	

Una birra e due cappuccini?
a ....

Un cappuccino e due caffè?
b ....

Un caffè e due bicchieri di vino?
c ....

Un'aranciata e due gelati?
d ....

now you're talking!

1　**1•62** Imagine you're in a bar in Pisa. You're going to order drinks at the **cassa** for yourself and two Italian friends.

- ◆ Ask Emilio what he'd like to drink.
- ● **Un bicchiere di vino bianco.**
- ◆ Now ask his sister, Francesca, what she'd like.
- ● **Un'aranciata, per favore.**

- ◆ At the **cassa**, greet the woman; order a glass of white wine, an orange drink and a beer.

For conversations 2, 3 and 4, make sure you know the words and phrases for the following situations, then close your book and be guided by the audio.

2　**1•63** You're offered a coffee.

- ◆ You accept, ask for a cappuccino and say *without sugar* when asked.

3　**1•64** Someone has asked what you'd like to drink.

- ◆ You ask what a milk shake is in Italian.

4　**1•65**
- ◆ When the waiter arrives, you order two glasses of wine and two beers.
- ◆ When he asks whether you would like red or white wine, say red.
- ◆ When the drinks arrive, thank the waiter. Say *Cheers!*

If you were in the same **caffè** with your family or colleagues or a group of friends, what drinks would you order for them?

quiz

1 Which of these is the odd one out?

   zucchero   aranciata   frullato   vino

2 Is coffee with alcohol **caffè macchiato** or **caffè corretto**?

3 If you wanted ice with your drink, would you order **con ghiaccio** or **senza ghiaccio**?

4 What are the plurals of **vino**, **birra**, **bicchiere**?

5 What is a **scontrino**?

6 Are nouns ending in **-o** generally masculine or feminine?

7 How do you say *Cheers!* in Italian?

8 If you order **acqua minerale gassata**, would you get still or sparkling water?

9 What two ways do you know of accepting a drink?

10 How do you say *You're welcome* in response to **Grazie**?

Now check whether you can ...

- order a drink in a bar
- offer someone a drink
- accept when someone offers you a drink
  ... or refuse politely
- say whether you want your drink with or without something
- ask what something is in Italian
- say *Cheers!*

Bring your Italian learning into your everyday life at every opportunity. Every time you have something to drink, think of the word in Italian. When buying a round of drinks, try to memorize the list in Italian.

In a restaurant, bar or supermarket, see how many drinks you can name in Italian.

Punto di controllo 1

1   **1•66** Listen to one of Fiorella's interviews for her survey, then tick the right information. Listen out for her first question:
    Lei è qui in vacanza o per lavoro? *Are you here on holiday or for work?*

Laura Santoro è in Italia	☐ in vacanza	☐ per lavoro
Laura è	☐ italiana	☐ americana
Suo padre è	☐ italiano	☐ americano
È in Italia con	☐ sua nonna	☐ suo padre
È di	☐ San Diego	☐ Santiago
È	☐ sposata	☐ divorziata
Ha	☐ due figli	☐ un figlio
È	☐ casalinga	☐ disoccupata

2   **1•67** While waiting at the airport, you overhear two students getting to know each other. Listen to their conversation and then fill in the missing details.

nome	nazionalità	età *age*	fratelli/sorelle
Caterina			
Jonathan			

3   **1•68** Caterina and Jonathan decide to have a drink together and go to the bar. Make a note of what they have to drink and the phone numbers which they exchange.

	un bicchiere di ...	numero di telefono
Caterina		
Jonathan		

4   **1•69** Practise pronouncing the names of these Italian wines, then check your pronunciation with the audio.

Chianti	**Frascati**	**Valpolicella**	**Barbaresco**
Tocai	**Verdicchio**	**Bardolino**	**Barolo**
Lambrusco	**Montepulciano d'Abruzzo**		**Soave**

5 **1•70** Listen to some of the interim results from the Eurovision Song Contest being read out and fill in the missing numbers.
Can you guess what all the countries are?

Danimarca	19	Lussemburgo	
Grecia	75	Norvegia	
Irlanda		Olanda	
Israele		Portogallo	

A good way to practise low numbers is to throw two dice and say aloud all the possible number combinations:

uno
cinque
quindici
cinquantuno

6 Choose the right expression.

Cin cin!

Bene, grazie.

Sì, grazie.

Scusi?

Piacere.

Prego.

a Accepting a drink.
b In reply to **grazie**.
c You haven't heard something properly.
d You're introduced to someone.
e In reply to **Come sta?**
f Saying *Cheers!*

7   The hotel **padrone** *proprietor* has asked if you would help his
    cousin fill in a form for an English course in London.
    What are the questions you would need to ask her before you could
    fill in the missing entries?

Name: _____

Address: Via Gramsci 23, 41100 MODENA

Telephone no: 059 933121

Age: _____

Nationality: Italian

Occupation: _____

a ....

b ....

c ....

8   Fill the gaps in these sentences.

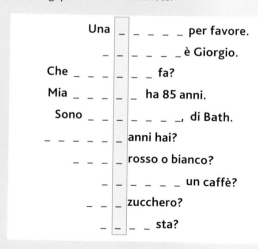

Una _ _ _ _ _ per favore.

_ _ _ _ _ _ è Giorgio.

Che _ _ _ _ _ _ fa?

Mia _ _ _ _ _ ha 85 anni.

Sono _ _ _ _ _ _ _, di Bath.

_ _ _ _ _ _ anni hai?

_ _ _ _ rosso o bianco?

_ _ _ _ _ _ un caffè?

_ _ _ zucchero?

_ _ _ _ sta?

What is the word in the shaded column?

9 A neighbour asks for your help when her daughter receives a letter in Italian from a penfriend. Translate the first page of the letter for them. Some words and expressions are given underneath; any other new vocabulary can be found in the glossary.

Siracusa

Cara Rachel,
mi chiamo Alessandra Giardi e sono siciliana, di Siracusa. Ho quattordici anni.

Siamo cinque in famiglia – mio padre, Massimo, che è disoccupato; mia madre, Giuseppina, che è infermiera all'ospedale; e mio fratello Stefano, che è studente. Stefano ha diciannove anni. C'è anche mia nonna,

> **siamo cinque** *we are five, there are five of us*
> **all'** *at the*
> **che** *who*
> **c'è** *there is*

Don't worry too much about making mistakes. You'll learn much more quickly if you try and express yourself, even if you make a few mistakes, than if you say nothing until you are word perfect.

You can give yourself time to think by using words such as **allora** *right, well then* or **vediamo** *let's see*.

Scusi, dov'è la stazione?

asking where something is

... and asking for help to understand

talking about where you live and work

In Italia ...

the focal point of many Italian towns is **il centro storico** *the old town*. Narrow streets and beautiful old buildings still remain much as they were centuries ago. In some towns, historic buildings house contemporary institutions such as **il municipio** *the town hall*, **l'azienda di turismo** or **l'ufficio turistico** *the tourist office*, **la Camera di Commercio** the *Chamber of Commerce* or **la questura** the *police headquarters*.

Asking where something is

1   **1•71** Listen to these key phrases.

Scusi.	Excuse me.
Dove?	Where?
Dov'è il duomo?	Where is the cathedral?
È lontano?	Is it far?
... dieci minuti a piedi.	... 10-minute walk.

2   **1•72** Mario asks his friend Anna to point out some local landmarks on his map. First check the meanings of the words using the glossary.

Now listen and match the buildings with the phrases below.

a   **qui** *here*

b   **dietro** *behind* **il municipio**

c   **lì** *over there*

d   **in via** *street* **della Vittoria**

e   **in centro città** *in the town centre*

In italiano ...

the words for *the* in the singular are:

masculine	**il**		**centro**	before a consonant
	l'	⎧ **ufficio**		before a vowel or **h**
		⎩ **hotel**		
	lo		**studio**	before **z** or **s** + consonant
feminine	**la**		**stazione**	before a consonant
	l'		**agenzia**	before a vowel

G3

... and asking for help to understand

3 **1•73** Listen to these key phrases.

Può ripetere, per favore?	Can you repeat that, please?
Può parlare lentamente?	Can you speak slowly?
Dove sono i negozi?	Where are the shops?
... a duecento metri.	... 200 metres away.
... a cinquecento metri.	... 500 metres away.

4 **1•74** Listen as Mario is stopped in the street by someone looking for **il municipio** the *town hall*. She finds it difficult to understand his reply. Assuming she understands English, can you interpret for her?

Visitor **Può parlare lentamente?**

Mario **È in centro, lontano da qui ... venti minuti a piedi.**

5 **1•75** Listen to someone asking where **i negozi** *the shops* are. How does she ask *Where are ...* ?

Listen again and make a note of these key points from the answer:
Where are they and how far away?
How long will it take to walk there?

In italiano ...

the words for *the* in the plural are:

masculine	i	negozi	before a consonant
	gli	⌠ uffici, hotel	before a vowel or **h**
		⌊ studi	before **z** or **s** + consonant
feminine	le	⌠ piazze	before a consonant
		⌊ aziende	before a vowel

G3

---

6 How would you ask where the following are?

- the tourist office
- the post office
- the station
- the shops

Talking about where you live

1   **1•76** Listen to these key phrases.

Dove abita?	Where do you live?
Abita qui?	Do you live here?
Abito ...	I live ...
... a Bologna.	... in Bologna.
... in centro.	... in the centre.
... in periferia.	... in the suburbs.
... in campagna.	... in the country.

2   **1•77** Mario asks some of the people he meets in Bologna where they live. Listen and tick who lives where.

	in centro	in periferia	in campagna
signora 1			
signore			
signora 2			

3   **1•78** Later, others talk to him about their homes. Listen and make a note of the numbers missing here from their addresses. In Italy, the number is usually written after the street name.

Claudia Bonino	**Viale Roma,** ....
Riccardo Quarta	**Piazza Garibaldi,** ....
Caterina Galli	**Via Verdi,** ....
La figlia di Caterina	**Via Aurelia,** ....

4   **1•78** Listen again to the last conversation, this time making a note of what type of house they all live in.

un appartamento *flat*	**un palazzo** *block of flats*
una casa *house*	**una villetta** *small detached house*

5   How would you say what type of house you live in and where it is?

... and work

6 1•79 Listen to these key phrases.

Dove lavora?	Where do you work? **(lei)**
Dove lavori?	Where do you work? **(tu)**
Lavoro ...	I work ...
Non lavoro.	I don't work.

7 1•80 Listen to Mario talking to Caterina Galli and her children Franca and Luciano. Decide who works:

in un ufficio *in an office* ....

per la Zanussi *for Zanussi* ....

In italiano ...

to show <u>who</u> is doing something you change the verb ending, instead of using words for *I, you, he*, etc.

	abit<u>are</u> *to live*	**lavor<u>are</u>** *to work*	**prend<u>ere</u>** *to take*
I	abit<u>o</u>	lavor<u>o</u>	prend<u>o</u>
you **(tu)**	abit<u>i</u>	lavor<u>i</u>	prend<u>i</u>
you **(lei)**	abit<u>a</u>	lavor<u>a</u>	prend<u>e</u>
he/she	abit<u>a</u>	lavor<u>a</u>	prend<u>e</u>

A very large number of Italian verbs end in **-are** and follow the same pattern as **abitare** and **lavorare**.

To say *I, you, we, <u>don't</u>* do something, you simply put **non** before the verb.

G5

---

8 1•81 Listen as five people answer the question **Dove lavora?** and number their answers 1 to 5 as you hear them. Can you work out what the fifth person does?

Lavoro in un ufficio.	▢	**A Roma.** ▢
Lavoro per la Fiat.	▢	**Non lavoro.** ▢
In una pizzeria in centro.	▢	

put it all together

1   Fill the gaps with the correct form of *the* – **il, la, l', i, gli** or **le**.

a   .... duomo   .... negozi   .... casa

b   .... stazione   .... azienda   .... appartamento

c   .... vino   .... acqua   .... birra

d   .... madre   .... padre   .... bambini

2   Match the answers to the questions.

a	Dov'è la stazione?	Cinque minuti a piedi.
b	Dove lavora?	È in centro.
c	Abita qui?	Sono in centro.
d	Dove sono i negozi?	No, lavoro in centro.
e	Lavora in periferia?	Lavoro in via Marconi.
f	Il museo è lontano?	Sì, abito qui.

3   In the last four pages there are examples of both **a** and **in** used with places to mean *in*. Can you work out which you would use with the following?

a   .... Firenze   e   .... un negozio

b   .... piazza Garibaldi   f   .... una pizzeria

c   .... Milano   g   .... un ufficio

d   .... via Manzini   h   .... Roma

4   Rearrange the letters to find the following:

a	a home	OMRATPNPAAET
b	a number	UOTEEDNC
c	a civic building	OIUCIMNPI
d	a word for *the*	IGL
e	part of a town	AFERRIPIE

now you're **talking!**

1   **1•82** Before leaving your hotel to see the city, you ask the
    receptionist where a few places are.

   ◆ Greet her and ask where the cathedral is.
   ● **Il Duomo? È in centro – in Piazza Duomo.**
   ◆ Ask if it's far.
   ● **No, no, dieci minuti a piedi.**
   ◆ Now ask her where the town hall is.
   ● **È dietro il Duomo.**
   ◆ You didn't quite catch that. Ask her to repeat what she said.

2   **1•83** Later, you're in the town hall.
   ◆ Ask the man at the entrance where the shops are.
   ● **Sono in via Michelangelo, a due passi.**
   ◆ Ask him to speak more slowly.
   ● **In via Michelangelo, a due passi … non è lontano.**
   ◆ Thank him.

3   **1•84** He asks you some questions. You might like to prepare
    your answers and then be guided by the audio. You'll need to
    know how to say:

   ◆ what nationality you are, and which town you live in
   ◆ whether you live in the town centre or out of town
   ◆ if you have a job, what you do and where you work

4   **1•85** You chat a little longer.
   ◆ Ask him if he lives here.
   ● **No, lavoro qui ma abito in via Belloni.**
   ◆ Ask where via Belloni is.
   ● **Non è lontano – è in periferia, a quindici minuti da qui.**

quiz

1 Is **qui** or **lì** the Italian for *here*?
2 What's the difference between **dov'è?** and **dove sono?**
3 If something is **dietro la stazione**, is it near, behind or opposite the station?
4 To say someone lives in the suburbs, would you say **abita in periferia** or **abita in centro**?
5 What are the words for *the* before **birra** **figlio** **Italia**?
6 What is the **centro storico** of an Italian town?
7 If 200 is **duecento** and 500 is **cinquecento**, what's 400 in Italian?
8 To say *I don't live here* what word is missing from ... **abito qui**?
9 What are the various possible meanings of **Dove abita**?
10 How do you say 350 in Italian?

Now check whether you can ...

- ask where something is
- ask if it's far
- ask someone to repeat something
- ask someone to speak slowly
- say where you live and where you work
- ask someone where they live and work

> Learning language patterns (i.e. grammar) allows you to manipulate a language and to say what you want to say without relying on set phrases.
>
> **Parlare** is the Italian for *to speak* and it follows exactly the same pattern as **abitare** and **lavorare**. So, to say what languages you speak, you use **parlo** followed by the language, for example: **Parlo inglese**, **non parlo francese**. The Italian words for languages are the same as the words for masculine nationalities on page 17.

C'è una banca qui vicino?

understanding what there is in town

... and when it's open

making simple enquiries

... and understanding directions

In Italia ...

there are more World Heritage Sites than in any other country in the world. The official tourism site **www.italia.it/en** is a major source of information for visitors, not only relating to places of interest but also to healthcare, transport and hospitality. You can download apps for every Italian region.

It's also worth visiting the local tourist office for local knowledge and to pick up a free **piantina** *map*, leaflets and timetables. Look out for the international sign for information and the IAT logo.

Understanding what there is in town

1   **2•01** Listen to these key phrases.

Ecco ...	Here's ...
C'è ...	There is ...
Non c'è ...	There isn't ...
Ci sono ...	There are ...
molti, molte	many (m pl/f pl)

2   Can you match the Italian words on the right with the English equivalents?
Many are very similar but others you may have to look up in the glossary.

(**Una trattoria** is a small family restaurant.)

una banca	market
un albergo	restaurant
un mercato	theatre
una stazione	supermarket
un supermercato	chemist's
un museo	swimming pool
una piscina	bank
una farmacia	station
un teatro	hotel
un ristorante	museum

In italiano ...

ne means *of them*; **ce n'è uno/a** *there is one (of them)*.

---

3   **2•02** Caterina Bossoli at the **ufficio turistico** tells visitors about some of the amenities **in città** *in town*. She mentions several of the places from the list above. Listen and tick them as you hear them.

4   **2•02** Listen again and decide whether the following are **vero** or **falso**.

	vero	falso
a **C'è una piscina.**		
b **C'è un teatro.**		
c **Il mercato è in centro.**		
d **Ci sono molti ristoranti.**		

... and when it's open

5 2•03 Listen to these key phrases.

È aperto ...	It's open ...
È chiuso ...	It's closed ...
... oggi.	... today.
... ogni giorno.	... every day.
... ogni lunedì.	... every Monday.

lunedì *Mon*	**giovedì** *Thurs*
martedì *Tue*	**venerdì** *Fri*
mercoledì *Wed*	**sabato** *Sat*
	domenica *Sun*

6 2•04 In the tourist office, Mario gains some useful information about local places as he waits in a queue. Listen, then fill the gaps.

La piscina è aperta ....

.... **e** .... **c'è un mercato in Piazza Marconi in centro.**

Il museo è chiuso ....; **è aperto** ...., ...
e ....

L'azienda di turismo è chiusa ....

In italiano ...

when describing places or objects, adjectives have to be masculine or feminine to agree with what they describe.

Il museo è apert<u>o</u>.   **La piscina è apert<u>a</u>.**   **G4**

Making simple enquiries

1 **2•05** Listen to these key phrases.

C'è ...?	Is there ...?
C'è una banca qui vicino?	Is there a bank near here?
Ci sono ristoranti?	Are there any restaurants?
Quando?	When?
Mi dispiace.	I'm sorry.
Non lo so.	I don't know.

sempre dritto

a sinistra **a destra**

2 **2•06** Listen as Anna asks in the bar if there's a phone and a toilet.
Tick the boxes which show where they are.

	qui	lì	in fondo *at the end*	a destra	a sinistra
il telefono					
la toilette					

3 **2•07** Later, she needs **una banca**. The first person she asks isn't from the area. How does he say he doesn't know?

4 **2•08** She tries again. Listen out for **poi** *then*.
Should she go left or right first?

5 **2•09** Next, the chemist's. Listen and make a note in English of the instructions. Listen out for **la prima a destra** *first on the right*.

....

....

... and understanding directions

6 **2•10** Listen as she then decides to find the **azienda di turismo**.

Where is it?
Is it open today?
What number **autobus** *bus* could she take?

7 **2•11** Anna decides to walk and asks again for directions. Listen as she's given two instructions.

How far is it to the **semaforo** *traffic lights*?
Should she turn right or left at the lights?

8 **2•12 L'ufficio è aperto.** Anna asks about markets, museums, swimming pools and **magazzini** *department stores*. Listen and choose **vero** or **falso** for each of the following.

		vero	falso
a	**C'è un mercato ogni giorno.**		
b	**Ci sono due musei.**		
c	**I musei sono chiusi domenica.**		
d	**La piscina è aperta mercoledì.**		
e	**I magazzini sono in centro.**		
f	**I magazzini sono chiusi giovedì.**		

In italiano ...

like nouns, adjectives have plural endings, both masculine and feminine.

I musei sono aperti.
Le piscine sono aperte.
Ci sono molti ristoranti e molte pizzerie.

G4

---

9 How would you ask if there's one of the following nearby?

- bank
- chemist's
- restaurant
- supermarket

put it all together

1   Read the following notices and answer the questions.

Galleria d'arte moderna
Via Flaminia, 16
aperta ogni giorno
9.00–19.00
domenica 9.00–13.00

Centro della Ceramica
Via S. Margherita, 4
Orario: 9.30–13.30
Chiuso martedì
Ingresso gratuito

APT
Azienda di Promozione Turistica
ogni giorno 9.00–13.30;
15.45–19.00

Museo Archeologico
Da martedì a sabato
9.00–17.00
domenica 9.00–12.00
lunedì chiuso
Ingresso € 3,00

a   On which day is the Archeological Museum closed?
b   Is the Gallery of Modern Art open on Sundays?
c   When is the tourist office open?
d   On which day is the Ceramics Centre closed?

2   Using **c'è, non c'è, ci sono** and **non ci sono**, say which of the amenities mentioned in this unit there are in your home town.

e.g. **C'è un teatro. Non c'è una piscina.**
You might need **un cinema**, which is masculine even though it ends in **-a**.

3   Say in Italian which days the following in your town are open and closed.

a   bank   b   library **(biblioteca)**   c   post office

now you're talking!

1   **2•13 In città**, you ask for some information from a man at the bus stop.

 ◆ Say *Excuse me* and ask if there's a chemist's nearby.
 ● **Una farmacia … Sì, a sinistra poi sempre dritto.**
 ◆ Repeat the directions you were given and thank him.

2   **2•14** This time you stop a woman who's passing.

 ◆ Say *Excuse me* and ask if there's a supermarket here.
 ● **C'è l'ipermercato a Molinella … ma è lontano.**
 ◆ Ask if there's a bus.
 ● **Sì, deve prendere il numero quarantadue.**
 ◆ Repeat the number of the bus, thank her and say goodbye.

3   **2•15** Imagine you've just arrived in Florence on the train.

 ◆ Ask if there's a bar nearby.
 ● **Lì a sinistra – ecco.**
 ◆ Say *thank you* and ask if there's a hotel nearby.
 ● **Mi dispiace, non lo so.**
 ◆ Ask where the tourist office is.
 ● **A destra, sempre dritto duecento metri, poi la prima a sinistra.**
 ◆ Repeat the instructions then ask if it's open.
 ● **Sì, sì.**

4   **2•16** Later you look for somewhere to eat.

 ◆ Ask if there are any restaurants nearby.
 ● **In via Doria c'è la Trattoria Corallo**.
 ◆ Ask if it's far.
 ● **No, no, cinque minuti a piedi.**

quiz

1 What would you expect to find in a building with an **IAT** logo on it?

2 If someone told you to go **a destra**, would you go left or right?

3 Can you name two eating places in Italian?

4 How would you ask if there's a phone?

5 If the **ufficio turistico** is **chiuso**, is it open or closed?

6 To ask if there's a supermarket, would you use **c'è** or **ci sono**?

7 Which two days of the week do not end in **-dì** in Italian?

8 What is **una piantina**?

9 How would you say you don't know?

10 What's the Italian for *department stores*?

Now check whether you can ...

- tell someone what there is in a town
- ask if something is available
- understand some straightforward directions
- ask if a place is open or closed
- say you're sorry
- say you don't know
- recognise the names of the days of the week

Learning a new language often involves guessing the meaning of words. Many Italian and English words derive from the same root, which makes it relatively easy to guess at their meaning with some confidence.

If **stazione** means *station* and **comunicazione** means *communication*, what do you think **nazione**, **tradizione** and **conversazione** mean?

Guessing, of course, is not always successful, but it's usually well worth a try.

Quanto costa?

understanding prices
... and asking for items in a shop
shopping for food in the market

In Italia ...

you will find a tremendous variety of places to shop ranging from bustling open-air markets for fresh produce to exclusive boutiques selling designer labels. Italy is famous particularly for fashion, leather goods, ceramics, wine and olive oil. Shop opening hours can vary according to where in Italy you are, but many close at lunchtime until around 3.30 p.m. and stay open until around 7.30 p.m.

La tabaccheria *the tobacconist's* sells all manner of useful items, including stamps and tickets for buses, trams and the metro.

Understanding prices

1   2•17 Listen to these prices in euros. You'll hear that **euro** does not change in the plural but that **centesimo** changes to **centesimi**.

€ 1,00	**un euro**	€ 3,99	**tre euro e novantanove**
€ 0,01	**un centesimo**	€ 50,00	**cinquanta euro**
€ 0,20	**venti centesimi**	€ 100,00	**cento euro**
€ 2,00	**due euro**	€ 250,00	**duecentocinquanta euro**

In Italia ...

the currency is the **euro €. 1 euro = 100 centesimi**. Prices are written with a comma between euros and **centesimi**: for example, **€ 12,20** is said as **dodici euro e venti**.

---

2   2•18 Make a note of the six prices you hear.

a € ....   b € ....   c € ....
d € ....   e € ....   f € ....

3   2•19 Listen to these key phrases.

Dica./Mi dica.	Can I help you?
Quanto costa?	How much is (it)?
questo/questa	this (m)/(f)
Quanto costano?	How much are (they)?
Avete ...?	Have you got ...?
Prendo ...	I'll take ...

4   2•20 Here's a list of items Mario needs from the **farmacia** chemist's, the **tabaccheria** and the **edicola** newspaper kiosk.
Can you find out what they are, using the glossary?

guida di Firenze
3 cartoline
giornale inglese
3 francobolli
carta telefonica
cerotti

... and asking for items in a shop

5   **2•21** Listen to the conversation in the **edicola,** then fill the gaps.

Commessa	**Buongiorno. Dica.**
Mario	**Signora, quanto** .... **questa guida?**
Commessa	.... **euro.**
Mario	**E quanto** .... **i giornali inglesi?**
Commessa	.... **e**..................

6   **2•22** Before listening to Mario in the **farmacia,** decide how you think he will ask how much the plasters cost.

7   **2•23** Next, to the **tabaccheria** to buy postcards and stamps for Britain and for the USA. Listen and find out how much things cost, then select the right answers.

una cartolina	un francobollo per la Gran Bretagna	un francobollo per gli Stati Uniti
€ 0,30	€ 0,40	€ 0,50
€ 0,41	€ 0,41	€ 0,51
€ 0,50	€ 0,49	€ 0,52

8   **2•24** Listen as Mario buys some **biglietti per l'autobus** *bus tickets.*

How much is one ticket?
How many does he buy?
How much change (**resto**) is he given?

9   How would you ask if the shop has:

- stamps?
- a guide?
- bus tickets?

... and how would you ask the price of:

- a postcard?
- bus tickets?
- an English newspaper?

Shopping for food

1

formaggio ½Kg

mezzo chilo

Zucchero 1Kg

un chilo

Olio 500ml

mezzo litro

Acqua 1 litro

un litro

panini

sei

Vino

una bottiglia

prosciutto 100g

100 grammi/un etto

2•25 Mario meets a friend, Barbara Gelli, shopping for food. Read her shopping list, then, as she tells Mario what she's going to buy, tick off the items.

She mentions one extra item. Can you add it to the list?

una bottiglia di vino rosso
un litro di acqua minerale (gassata)
mezzo litro di olio di oliva (extra vergine)
un chilo di zucchero
mezzo chilo di formaggio
un etto di prosciutto
6 panini

2   **2•26** Listen to these key phrases.

Mi dà ...	Could you give me ...?
Vorrei ...	I'd like ...
questi/queste	these (m)/(f)
Altro?	Anything else?
Basta così?	Is that all?
Basta.	That's enough./That's all.

3   **2•27** Listen as signora Gelli buys things from the various stalls and make a note of what she buys. After listening several times, match your list with the original one above. What hasn't she bought yet?

... in the market

banane pesche funghi cipolle

mele fragole patate pomodori

4   **2•28** She then goes to buy **frutta e verdura** *fruit and vegetables.*
Listen and decide what quantities of the following she buys:

● apples .... ● mushrooms .... ● tomatoes ....

5   **2•29** While waiting for Barbara, Mario listens to the people around
him shopping. Listen too and fill the gaps.

● **Vorrei mezzo chilo di questi** ....
● **Prendo** .... **banane.**
● **Mi dà** .... **di patate.**
● **Una di queste** .... **per favore.**

6   **2•30** Finally, listen as Barbara checks whether she has remembered
everything before going home. Has she got all the following?

▢ wine   ▢ mineral water   ▢ bread rolls   ▢ ham   ▢ cheese

What has she bought which was not on the original list?

7   How would you ask for:

● ½ kg of these apples?   ● three peaches?
● a litre of mineral water?   ● a bottle of red wine?

put it all together

1   Match the English with the Italian phrases:

a	Vorrei ...	How much is it?
b	Mi dà ...	That's all.
c	Basta così.	How much are they?
d	Quanto costa?	Do you have ...?
e	Avete ...?	Could you give me ...?
f	Altro?	I'd like ...
g	Quanto costano?	Anything else?

2   The following ingredients for **pizza** and for **macedonia**
     fruit salad have been mixed up. Sort these words into the
     appropriate columns – seven items in each.

	pizza	macedonia

fragole, arance, pomodori,
funghi, zucchero, patate,
pesche, formaggio
(mozzarella), banane,
mele, sale, pepe, olio di
oliva, farina, limone

....
....
....
....
....
....
....

Which ingredient is left over?

3   You are shopping for a picnic lunch – you want:

bread rolls, cheese, ham, tomatoes, bananas, apples,
two bottles of wine and a bottle of mineral water

Write your shopping list in Italian.

4   If you buy three items each costing the following, and pay
     for them all with a 50 euro note, how much change should
     you expect?

**diciotto euro, quattordici euro e venticinque, dieci euro e
settantacinque**

now you're **talking!**

Imagine you're in the market in Bologna, buying a picnic lunch.

1   2•31 First, **frutta e verdura**.

- **Buongiorno. Dica.**
- ◆ Ask for a kilo of apples and half a kilo of bananas.
- **Altro?**
- ◆ You want half a kilo of tomatoes.
- **Basta?**
- ◆ Say yes, that's all and thank him.

2   2•32 In the **alimentari** *grocer's* …

- ◆ Ask for four bread rolls.
- **E poi?**
- ◆ Say you'd like a bottle of red wine and a litre of sparkling mineral water.
- **Altro?**
- ◆ You'd like 100 grams of ham.
- **Quale?**
- ◆ He's asking which one. Say *This one here*.
- **Basta così?**
- ◆ Say that's all and thank him.

3   2•33 Then you go to the **tabaccheria**. Read the following notes, then close your book and be guided by the audio. You will need to:

- ◆ ask how much a stamp for Britain costs
- ◆ say you'll take two postcards and two stamps
- ◆ ask how much bus tickets cost
- ◆ buy six tickets
- ◆ ask for a telephone card

quiz

1 Would you use **Quanto costa?** or **Quanto costano?** to ask the price of: **le mele, i cerotti, una bottiglia di vino**?

2 How much is **cinquecentocinquantacinque**?

3 How many **etti** are there in a **chilo**?

4 Where can you buy bus tickets?

5 If **un giornale inglese** is an English newspaper, what is the Italian for an Italian newspaper?

6 How would you ask for a stamp for Australia?

7 To say *these tomatoes*, do you need **questi** or **queste**?

8 What word would you add to say *half a kilo*: .... **chilo**?

9 How would you say € 25,50 and € 76,95?

10 And how would you write in figures **ottantadue euro e quindici**?

Now check whether you can ...

- ask how much something costs
- understand the answer
- say you'd like something or you'll take something
- give some detail of what you want to buy,
  e.g. ask for a kilo, half a kilo, 100 grams of food, a bottle, a litre, half a litre of a liquid
- ask for stamps for a particular country

Looking things up in a dictionary can be more complicated than using the glossary and it is useful to know some basic grammatical terms and abbreviations. You'll find something like this:

orange 1 n *(fruit)* arancia f; *(tree)* arancio m; 2 adj *(colour)* arancione
organise v organizzare

Key: n = noun, f = feminine, m = masculine, adj = adjective, v = verb

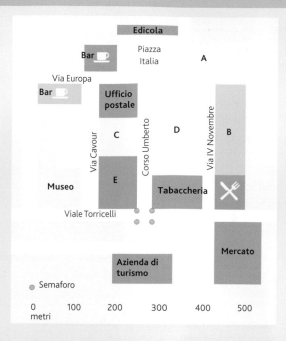

1 **2•34** Listen to three people in the **azienda di turismo** being given directions. Follow their route on the map, then write down the place they're looking for and the letter which corresponds to it on the map.

a .... b .... c ....

2 Look at the map again and decide which word fits in the gap in each sentence.

> azienda di turismo   edicola   bar   farmacia

a C'è un .... e c'è un' .... in piazza Italia.

b L' .... è a sinistra del mercato.

c La .... è fra la banca e l'ufficio postale.

3　**2●35** Listen to the assistant in the tourist office telling someone how far various Italian cities are from Milan, and fill in the distances.

Roma　　　　　................ **km da Milano**
Firenze　　　　................ **km**
Napoli　　　　　................ **km**
Bari　　　　　　................ **km**

4　**2●36** Listen and check whether the prices you hear are the same as the ones on the list. Identify the ones that are correct and change the ones which are wrong.

100g prosciutto di Parma	**€ 3,60**
1 litro olio di oliva extra vergine	**€ 8,95**
100g olive	**€ 2,25**
½kg pomodori	**€ 0,90**
pane integrale	**€ 1,00**
250g mozzarella	**€ 3,79**

5　Match each sentence to the place in which you're most likely to hear it.

> **Farmacia**　　**Tabaccheria**　　**Ufficio turistico**
> **Mercato**　　**Caffè**　　　　**Edicola**

a　**Quanto costano i giornali inglesi?**
b　**Mi dà mezzo chilo di mele.**
c　**Avete aspirina?**
d　**Vorrei tre francobolli.**
e　**È aperto oggi il museo?**
f　**Due birre, per favore.**

6　Unscramble the anagrams to find:

a　a day of the week　　　　　NAMOCEDI
b　something you buy in the **farmacia**　　TIOCRTE
c　a place to live　　　　　　LLAVI
d　a vegetable　　　　　　　TATAPA

7 Which one would you use …

> Può ripetere per favore?

> Non sono di qui.

> Come si dice in italiano?

> Mi dispiace.

> Non lo so.

> Può parlare lentamente?

a … when someone's speaking too quickly?
b … to explain you're not from the area?
c … if you don't know something?
d … to find out how to say something in Italian?
e … when you'd like to hear something again?
f … to say you're sorry?

8 Make the connection – match a word from A with one from B.

A	B
formaggio	casa
euro	lavoro
piscina	giornale
ristorante	pizza
francobollo	acqua
appartamento	banca
edicola	trattoria
professione	cartolina

9 Fill the gaps with **questo**, **questa**, **questi** or **queste**.

a **Mi dà mezzo chilo di ………… funghi.**
b **Quanto costa ………… cartolina?**
c **Vorrei due bottiglie di ………… vino rosso.**
d **Quanto costano ………… pesche?**
e **È aperto ………… ristorante?**
f **Prendo duecentocinquanta grammi di ………… fragole.**

10 Read Chris's postcard to Elena and decide whether the statements which follow are **vero** or **falso**.

Cara Elena,

Sono qui vicino a Rapallo in vacanza! L'albergo ha una piscina e un campo da tennis, e ci sono negozi, teatri, cinema e musei in centro città (non è lontano e c'è l'autobus).

Stefano arriva venerdì – lavora in un negozio da lunedì a giovedì. Sabato andiamo a Firenze.

Saluti   Chris

Sig.ra ROSSI Elena
Via Michelangelo, 20
41101 MODENA

		vero	falso
a	Chris lavora a Rapallo.	☐	☐
b	L'albergo è in centro.	☐	☐
c	C'è una piscina in albergo.	☐	☐
d	Elena arriva venerdì.	☐	☐
e	Stefano lavora mercoledì.	☐	☐
f	Elena abita a Modena.	☐	☐
g	Stefano è studente all'università.	☐	☐

11 Practise answering aloud the following questions about yourself. Why not record an 'interview' with yourself?

Come ti chiami?
Dove abiti?
Lavori? Che lavoro fai? Dove lavori? Lavori ogni giorno?
Sei inglese? Di dove sei?
Qual è il tuo numero di telefono?
Parli francese … tedesco … italiano … inglese?

Vorrei una camera

checking in at reception

finding a hotel room

booking ahead by phone

making requests

In Italia ...

you'll find a wide choice of places to stay, ranging from the basic
pensione *one-star hotel/guesthouse* to exclusive **hotel cinque stelle di
lusso** *luxury 5-star hotels*.

If you don't book beforehand, local tourist offices can supply lists and will
often check availability. The price of **una camera** *a hotel room* is on display
in the room, usually on the back of the door. This price is quoted **tutto
incluso** *all inclusive* which means that it includes tax and service charges
but not **la prima colazione** *breakfast*. Many people opt to have breakfast
in a bar.

Checking in at reception

1   2•37 Listen to these key phrases.

Ho prenotato ...	I've booked ...
una camera singola	
una camera doppia ... **a due letti** **matrimoniale**	
con bagno	
con doccia	

al terzo piano	on the third floor
al secondo/primo piano	on the second/first floor
al pianterreno	on the ground floor
Il suo nome?	Your name?
Il suo passaporto, **per favore.**	Your passport, please.

2   2•38 Maria Cavalleri is in reception at the Albergo Giotto. Listen as she greets the guests and checks their name in the register before giving them their key (**la chiave**). Listen several times, then fill in the details missing from the grid below.

	sing dopp./mat. dopp./2 letti	bagno doccia	numero della camera	piano
sig. Pittara				
sig.ra Rossini				
sig. Barucci				

3   2•38 Listen again and make a note of where **l'ascensore** *the lift* is.

....

Finding a hotel room

1   **2•39** Listen to these key phrases.

Vorrei una camera …	I'd like a room …
… per stasera.	… for tonight.
… per tre notti.	… for three nights.
… per una settimana.	… for a week.
fino a …	until …
Come si scrive?	How do you spell it?

2   **2•40** Two men arrive at the hotel reception without reservations. What does Maria say to check that the first man wants a room for tonight only? How long does the second man want to stay?

3   **2•41** Listen to Alberto saying the Italian alphabet and then spelling out his own name. What is his **cognome**?

A B C D E F G H I L M N O P Q R S T U V Z

In italiano …

  j (i lunga), k (cappa), w (doppia vu), x (ics) and y (ipsilon) are not in the Italian alphabet but are used to spell foreign words.

---

4   **2•42** Now listen to the whole of the conversation between Maria and the two men and note down their names.

  a ……………..   b ……………..

5   Now practise spelling your own name in Italian.

6   How would you say you'd like the following?

  • for tonight   • for a week

  • for 3 nights   • until Sunday

Booking ahead by phone

1 **2•44** Listen to these key phrases.

Pronto.	Hello. (on the telephone)
Un attimo.	One moment.
Vorrei prenotare una camera.	I'd like to book a room.
Per quando?	When for?
Siamo al completo.	We're full.

> **In italiano ...**
>
> dates are expressed with the number (*two*, *eleven*, *twenty-seven*, etc.) and the month. They start with **il**:
>
> | | |
> |---|---|
> | **il quindici giugno** | *15th June* |
> | **il ventisette agosto** | *27th August* |
> | **fino al dodici maggio** | *until 12th May* |
> | **dal 30 luglio al 6 agosto** | *from 30th July to 6th August* |
>
> The only exception is the first of the month, which is **il primo**:
>
> | | |
> |---|---|
> | **il primo marzo** | *1st March* |

2 **2•45** The receptionist is taking three bookings over the phone. Listen and work out the dates these people want rooms for.

a ....   b ....   c ....

Making requests

1   **2•46** Listen to these key phrases.

Posso ... /Possiamo ...   Can I ... /Can we ...
... vedere la camera?   ... see the room?
... pagare con la carta di credito?   ... pay by credit card?
... lasciare la valigia qui?   ... leave the suitcase here?
... telefonare da qui?   ... telephone from here?
... parcheggiare qui?   ... park here?

2   **2•47** Some of the guests are leaving while others are arriving, and each one asks the receptionist if they can do something.
As you listen, can you work out who wants to do what?

signor Belloni	leave a suitcase in the hotel
Lorna Tonino	make a telephone call
Luigi Ciani	pay by credit card
signor Chini	speak to the manager
	see the room on offer

In italiano ...

the verb which follows **posso** and **possiamo** is always in the infinitive. This is the form you find in the dictionary, ending in -are, -ere or -ire.   **G9**

---

3   **2•48** A couple arriving at the hotel are unsure where to leave their car.
Listen to their conversation and decide:

- where they are advised to park
- what their **targa** *car registration number* is

Parcheggio

put it **all together**

1   Match the Italian with the English.

a	**Vorrei prenotare ...**	Can I ...?
b	**Ho prenotato ...**	I'd like to book ...
c	**Avete ...?**	I've booked ...
d	**Posso ...?**	Hello.
e	**Possiamo ...?**	Have you got ...?
f	**Pronto.**	Can we ...?

2   Complete the following:

a   **Ho prenotato** ....

b   **Vorrei** ....

c   **Avete** ....?

d   **Ha** ....? **(1 notte)**

e   **Vorrei prenotare** .... **(21 marzo)**

f   **Posso** ....?

Hotel Astoria ★ ★ ★ ★
Via Aquila Nera, 22 Tel: 035/938045
- 28 camere con servizi privati, aria condizionata, TV
- parcheggio privato
- vicino al centro storico
- chiuso 30 novembre – 1 marzo

3   If you asked the proprietors of the Hotel Astoria the
    following questions, would they answer **sì** or **no**?

	sì	no
a **C'è un ristorante?**		
b **Possiamo parcheggiare?**		
c **Avete una piscina?**		
d **L'albergo è lontano dal centro città?**		
e **È aperto in gennaio?**		

now you're talking!

1 **2•49** Take the part of Anna Mannoni arriving at the Hotel Giotto.

- **Buongiorno, signora. Mi dica.**
- ◆ Ask if they have a room.
- **Singola o doppia?**
- ◆ Say single, with bathroom.
- **Per quante notti?**
- ◆ Say for tonight.
- **Va bene, signora – camera numero 245 al secondo piano.**
- ◆ Ask if you can see the room.
- **Certo, signora.**

2 **2•50** Now take the part of John Graham.

- ◆ Greet the receptionist and say you've booked a room.
- **Il suo nome, signore?**
- ◆ Tell her who you are.
- **Allora, una camera doppia con bagno.**
- ◆ This isn't what you booked. Say no, a single room with bath.
- **... per tre notti?**
- ◆ Say no, for two nights – until 22nd August.
- **Che strano. Come si scrive il suo nome?**
- ◆ Spell out Graham.
- **Ah signore – sì, scusi – camera singola per due notti.**
- ◆ Ask if you can pay by credit card.
- **Sì, certo.**

quiz

1 Name two things in a hotel beginning with **c**.

2 Which month follows **luglio**?

3 Which date is **il primo maggio**?

4 What is **il primo piano**?

5 What is **la prima colazione**?

6 If someone asked you for your **targa**, what information would you give them?

7 When would you use **posso** and when **possiamo**?

8 If you were quoted a price **tutto incluso** in a hotel, would you assume breakfast was included?

9 **Albergo** is another word for **hotel**. What do you add to say *4-star hotel*?

10 If **vorrei vedere** means *I'd like to see*, what's the Italian for *I'd like to pay by credit card* and *I'd like to phone*?

Now check whether you can ...

- say you've booked a room
- ask for a room in a hotel and specify single or double
- say whether you want a room with or without a bath or shower
- say how long you want the room for and specify dates
- ask to see the room
- ask if you can pay by credit card
- spell your name in Italian

If you travel to Italy with someone else you might prefer to say 'we ... ' rather than 'I ... '. For nearly all verbs, this involves substituting the **-o** ending with **-iamo**:

posso	**possiamo**
abito *I live*	**abitiamo** *we live*

There are a few exceptions, of course. Look out for **siamo** *we are* and **abbiamo** *we have*.

A che ora parte?

asking about public transport

finding out train times

buying tickets

... and checking travel details

In Italia ...

public transport is generally cheap and reliable and an excellent way to see the country. There are **treni** *trains*, **pullman** *coaches* and, to and from the many Italian islands, **traghetti** *ferries* and **aliscafi** *hydrofoils*.

In town, **autobus** *buses* are cheap and frequent and some towns also have a tram system. **Roma**, **Milano** and **Napoli** have a **metro** *underground*.

The rail network **Trenitalia** (www.trenitalia.com) operates a range of trains, from the premier high-speed **Frecciarossa** *Red Arrow* to much slower local trains. For long-distance trains you have to buy a ticket in advance; and some incur a **supplemento** *extra charge*.

Asking about public transport

1   **2•51** Listen to these key phrases.

C'è un autobus per ...?	Is there a bus to ...?
C'è un pullman per ...?	Is there a coach to ...?
Quando parte?	When does it leave?
Ce n'è uno ...	There's one ...
... alle dieci.	... at 10 o'clock.
... ogni ora.	... every hour.
... ogni mezz'ora.	... every half hour.

In italiano ...

to say what time something takes place, the key word is **alle**:

alle due | 02:00 | **alle dieci** | 10:00 | **alle diciannove** | 19:00 |

The 24-hour clock is universally used with travel times.

---

2   **2•52** Listen to three queries at the **ufficio informazioni** *information office* and tick the frequency of the services and the next departure times. The first one has been done for you.

	Ce n'è uno ogni ...			Parte alle ...		
	½ ora	ora	2 ore	7.00	10.00	11.00
L'autobus per la stazione	✓				✓	
L'autobus per piazza Garibaldi						
Il pullman per l'aeroporto						

3   How would you ask if there is:

- a coach to the airport?
- a bus to the station?
- one at 10 o'clock?

Finding out train times

1 **2•53** Listen to these key phrases.

A che ora ...	What time ...
parte il prossimo treno ...	does the next train leave ...
... per Roma?	... for Rome?
A che ora ...	What time ...
arriva il treno ...	does the train arrive ...
... a Roma?	... in Rome?
... da Roma?	... from Rome?

In italiano ...

hours are separated from minutes by **e** *and*:

alle nove e venti at 09.20

alle quattordici e cinquantadue at 14.52

---

2 **2•54** Listen to people enquiring about trains to various cities and fill in the missing departure and arrival times.

PARTENZE *departures*
Roma ....
Bologna ....
Bergamo ....

ARRIVI *arrivals*
Venezia ....
Padova ....

3 **2•54** Listen again and decide **vero** or **falso** for the following:

                          vero   falso

a **C'è un treno per Bologna ogni ora.** ☐ ☐

b **Il treno arriva a Bergamo alle 10.55.** ☐ ☐

4 How would you ask what time:

- the next train leaves for Florence?
- it arrives in Florence?
- the train arrives from Venice?

Buying tickets

1   2•55 Listen to these key phrases.

Un biglietto per ...	A ticket for ...
Andata ...	Single ...
... o andata e ritorno?	... or return?
prima classe	first class
seconda classe	second class
con supplemento	with a supplement
Da che binario parte?	Which platform does it leave from?

2   2•56 Listen to several people buying train tickets and indicate in the grid what kind of ticket they buy.

	Biglietto		Classe		Supplemento	
	andata	andata e ritorno	1a	2a	sì	no
Bologna						
Milano						
Verona						
Firenze						
Roma						

3   2•56 Listen again to the last recording. The **bigliettaio** *ticket clerk* tells two of the people buying tickets which platform their trains will leave from. Make a note of their destinations and the platform numbers.

	Treno per	Binario numero
a	....	....
b	....	....

... and checking travel details

4 2•57 Listen to these key phrases.

È diretto?	Is it a through train?
Devo ...?	Do I have to ...?
Deve ...	You have to ...
... cambiare	... change
... andare	... go
... prenotare il posto	... make a seat reservation
... scendere	... get off (a train or bus)
Non capisco.	I don't understand.

5 2•58 Listen as passengers check the details of their journey in the **ufficio informazioni** and tick the correct information. The first is travelling to **Napoli**.

Deve cambiare?   **Sì**　　 **No**

6 2•59 The next passenger, travelling to Arezzo, has difficulty with the information he's being given. He speaks English – act as interpreter and tell him:

- what time his train leaves
- whether he has to change
- the cost of the ticket
- any other information he needs to know

7 2•60 Listen as Mario is given some information about bus tickets and bus stops (**fermate**), and then fill the gaps with **devo** or **deve**.

Mario	**Dove posso comprare un biglietto per l'autobus?**
signora	.... **andare in tabaccheria – ce n'è una lì, a destra.**
Mario	**Grazie.**
Mario	**Scusi, ... scendere qui per il Duomo?**
signora 2	**No, alla prossima fermata.**
Mario	**Grazie.**

put it all together

1   Select the answer for each question.

a	C'è un treno diretto per Napoli?
b	A che ora parte il prossimo treno per Padova?
c	A che ora arriva questo treno a Chiusi?
d	Devo prenotare il posto?
e	C'è un pullman per Verona?
f	Dove posso comprare i biglietti per l'autobus?
1	In edicola o in tabaccheria.
2	No, deve cambiare a Roma.
3	Sì, deve prenotare per l'Intercity.
4	Ce n'è uno ogni due ore e mezza.
5	Parte alle nove e venticinque.
6	Alle quindici e dodici.

2   Work out how you would say the following in Italian, using the 24-hour clock:

a   at 7 a.m.   d   at 11 p.m.
b   at 7 p.m.   e   at 8.25 a.m.
c   at 11 a.m.   f   at 8.25 p.m.

3   Choose the correct ending for each sentence.

a	Mi dà un biglietto di	venti minuti.
b	C'è un autobus ogni	nove e venti.
c	Deve scendere alla	ventidue euro.
d	Il prossimo treno parte alle	seconda classe.
e	Il biglietto costa	seconda fermata.

4   How would you finish the question: **Devo** ....?

a   to find out if you have to change
b   to ask if a seat reservation is necessary
c   to ask if you have to get off the bus here

now you're talking!

1   **2•61** Imagine you're staying in Umbria and want to see the area using public transport. First, to the coach station.

- ◆ Ask the woman in the office if there's a coach to Perugia.
- ● **Ce n'è uno ogni due ore.**
- ◆ Ask what time the next coach leaves.
- ● **Alle dieci.**
- ◆ Find out if you have to make a seat reservation.
- ● **No, non è necessario.**
- ◆ Ask how much the ticket costs.
- ● **Andata o andata e ritorno?**
- ◆ Say a return.
- ● **Quattordici euro.**

2   **2•62** Next, to Orvieto by train.

- ◆ Ask the man in the ticket office what time the next train leaves for Orvieto.
- ● **Orvieto ... alle nove e quaranta.**
- ◆ Find out what time it arrives in Orvieto.
- ● **Alle dieci e quarantasette.**
- ◆ Ask if you have to change.
- ● **No, è diretto.**
- ◆ Say you'd like a return ticket.
- ● **Prima o seconda classe?**
- ◆ Say second class, then ask which platform the train leaves from.
- ● **Binario numero quattro**.
- ◆ Thank him.

3   **2•63** Finally, by bus to the town centre. You meet a woman at the bus stop. You want to ask her the following:

- ◆ the time of the next bus
- ◆ if there's a **tabaccheria** nearby

quiz

1 To say *every ten minutes*, what word will you need to add?
   .... **dieci minuti**.

2 How do you say you don't understand?

3 What's the **Frecciarossa** and what does the word mean?

4 If someone starts their sentence to you with **Deve**, what are they telling you?

5 What time does something start if it starts **alle diciotto**?

6 Is **un biglietto di andata e ritorno** a single or a return ticket?

7 If you hear an announcement about **il treno da Roma**, is it about the train from Rome or to Rome?

8 What are **un traghetto** and **un aliscafo**?

9 Given that <u>we</u> *have to* is **dobbiamo,** what's the Italian for *Do we have to change*?

10 How would you say in Italian *I'd like to go to Florence tonight*?

Now check whether you can ...

- ask if there's a bus or a coach going to a particular place
- find out when it leaves
- ask what time trains (or other means of transport) depart and arrive
- find out what platform a train leaves from
- find out whether you have to make a seat reservation
- ask for a single or return ticket
- ask if you have to change
- say you don't understand

When learning a language, it can be very easy to underestimate how much you know. Go back occasionally to one of the early units to prove to yourself how much you've learnt. Think also about what you find easy ... and difficult. If you can identify your strengths and weaknesses, you can build on your strengths and find ways of compensating for the weaknesses.

Buon appetito!

reading the menu

asking about items on the menu

ordering a meal

saying what you like and don't like

... and paying compliments

In Italia ...

the best place to eat is the one full of local people, away from the main tourist spots. You can generally eat just as well in a small, family-run **trattoria** as in a smart **ristorante** – and pay a lot less.

Italian cooking makes use of fresh local produce and varies greatly from region to region. Look out for the words **specialità della regione** *local speciality* and **cucina casalinga** or **cucina casareccia** *home cooking*.

Il pranzo is the main meal of the day, served between midday and around 2.30 p.m. **La cena** *dinner, supper*, is generally a lighter meal than the **pranzo**. At the start of a meal, it's customary to wish people **Buon appetito!** *Enjoy your meal!*

Antipasti
Antipasto della casa

Starters, usually cold meats, cheese, seafood, olives and various vegetables.

Primi (piatti)
Zuppa del giorno
Minestrone
Tagliatelle al ragù/al pomodoro
Cannelloni al forno
Risotto alla marinara

First courses, usually soup, pasta or risotto

Secondi (piatti)
Bistecca alla griglia
Filetto di maiale ai funghi
Agnello arrosto
Petto di pollo all'aglio
Pesce del giorno

Second courses, usually **carne** *meat*, **pesce** *fish* or poultry

Contorni
Zucchini, Spinaci, Carote, Broccoli
Patate ~ fritte o arrosto
Insalata ~ verde o mista

Side dishes of vegetables or salad

Dessert
Frutta di stagione
Gelati assortiti
Sorbetto alla fragola
Torta della casa
Tiramisù
Formaggi assortiti della regione

Also referred to as **dolci**

pane e coperto

Bread and cover charge

Reading the menu

1   Read the menu and see how much of it you already
    understand or can guess.

2   Now read through the following notes, then go back and read the
    menu again. You may also need to consult the glossary.

    Some of the terms you find in a menu are very general.

    ... **del giorno**   *... of the day*
    ... **della casa**   *the house ...*
    ... **della regione**   *local ...*
    ... **di stagione**   *... in season*
    ... **misto**   *mixed ...*
    ... **assortiti**   *an assortment of ...*

    Others, starting with **al**, **alla**, **all'**, **alle**, **ai** or **agli**, are more precise
    and refer to the main ingredient of a dish, the way it is cooked or to a
    particular tradition.

    al pomodoro *with tomato*   **alla griglia** *grilled/barbecued*
    all'aglio *with garlic*   **ai ferri** *grilled/barbecued*
    ai funghi *with mushrooms*   **al forno** *baked*
    alla marinara *with seafood*   **allo spiedo** *on a spit*
    al ragù *with bolognese sauce*   **alla romana** *Roman style*

    Fish is usually fresh and often referred to on the menu simply as
    pesce del giorno.

    Meat is usually **manzo** *beef*, **agnello** *lamb*, **vitello** *veal* or **pollo**
    chicken but you can also find **coniglio** *rabbit*, **capretto** *goat* and
    cinghiale *wild boar*. It can be served as described above, or possibly:

    arrosto *roasted*   **fritto** *fried*
    in umido *stewed*   **bollito, lesso** *boiled*

Asking about items on the menu

1   2•64 Listen to these key phrases.

Cos'è ...?   What is ...?
Com'è ...?   What's ... like?
Come sono ...?   What are ... like?

2   2•65 In the Trattoria Chiezzi, Emilio the waiter shows some people to their table (**tavolo**). How many of them are there?
What do they order as an **aperitivo**?

3   2•66 Emilio tells them what there is for the **primo piatto**. Some of the items are on the menu on page 88. As you hear these, put a tick by them.

4   2•67 Listen as they ask Emilio some questions about the dishes. What is the soup of the day?
Can you identify two ingredients missing from this recipe for
spaghetti alla carbonara?

> **Spaghetti alla carbonara**
> Ingredienti:
>
> spaghetti
> uova *eggs*
> ....
> panna *cream*
>
> ....
> pepe *pepper*

In italiano ...

because pasta dishes are plural – i cannelloni, gli spaghetti, le tagliatelle, le lasagne, etc. – you say **Come sono?** not **Com'è?** to ask what a pasta dish is like.

G9

5   How would you ask what the following are like?

- risotto
- ravioli

Ordering a meal

1 **2•68** Listen to these key phrases.

Pronto/a/i/e per ordinare?	Ready to order?
Cosa prende/prendono?	What will you have?
Cosa consiglia?	What do you recommend?
Da bere?	To drink?
Prendo …	I'll have …
Niente … per me.	No … for me.

2 **2•69** A couple with their daughter order their **primo piatto**.
Listen to the conversation, then fill the gaps.

signore .... **il minestrone.**
signora **Io** .... **il risotto ai funghi, e le**
  tagliatelle al ragù .... **mia figlia.**

3 **2•70** A woman eating alone at the next table skips the **primo**. Listen
to her ordering a **secondo piatto** and a **contorno** and tick what she
chooses from this menu.

Primi	zuppa di verdura
	lasagne al forno
Secondi	pesce del giorno
	filetto di maiale
	agnello arrosto con aglio e rosmarino
Contorni	broccoli, piselli, zucchini, patate,
	insalata

4 **2•71** Listen as she orders something to drink.
Does she want sparkling or still water?
Does she order red or white wine?
Does she have ½ litre or ¼ litre?

5 How would you say you'll have the fish and a salad?

Saying what you like and don't like

1   2•72 Listen to these key phrases.

Vorrei assaggiare ...	I'd like to taste ...
Mi piace ...	I like ...
Non mi piace ...	I don't like ...
Le piace ...?	Do you like ...? **(lei)**
Ti piace ...?	Do you like ...? **(tu)**
È buono/buonissimo.	It's good/extremely good.

2   2•73 One table has finished their **secondo**. Listen as the man calls Emilio over. What does he say to attract Emilio's attention? Tick which of the following they are offered for dessert.

mele	melone	fragole
formaggio	gelato	yogurt
torta di mele	torta al cioccolato	tiramisù

3   2•74 Listen as Emilio brings the desserts over and decide who likes and who doesn't like the **dolcelatte** – a local cheese.

	mi piace	non mi piace
signora 1		
signore		
signora 2		

In italiano ...

to say something is extremely ... or very ..., you can add **-issimo** to the adjective minus its final vowel.

il formaggio è buon<u>o</u>	buonissimo
la torta è buon<u>a</u>	buonissima
i gelati sono buon<u>i</u>	buonissimi
le fragole sono buon<u>e</u>	buonissime

---

4   How would you say you like ...   • white wine?   • cheese?

... and paying compliments

5   **2•76** Listen to these key phrases.

Tutto bene?	Is everything all right?
Complimenti!	Congratulations!
È delizioso!	It's delicious!
Le piacciono ...	Do you like ...
... i formaggi italiani?	... Italian cheeses?
Mi piacciono ...	I like ...
... tutti i formaggi.	... all cheeses.

6   **2•77** The **padrone** *owner* of the Trattoria Chiezzi comes into the dining room to ask if everything is all right. Tick any of the following which you hear.

In italiano ...

to talk about liking something which is plural, you replace **piace** with **piacciono**:

Le piacciono i cannelloni?	*Do you like cannelloni?*
Sì, mi piacciono.	*Yes, I like them.*
Ti piacciono le cipolle?	*Do you like onions?*
No, non mi piacciono molto.	*No, I don't like them much.*

---

7   **2•78** The family is ready for dessert. What do they all (**tutti**) choose?

8   How would you say you like ...

- strawberries?
- apples?

put it all together

1   Match the Italian with the English.

a	della casa	baked
b	alla griglia	with tomatoes
c	fritto	of the day
d	di stagione	of the house
e	del giorno	in season
f	al forno	grilled
g	al pomodoro	fried

2   Sort the following dishes into the appropriate columns.

patate coniglio gelato risotto ravioli vitello
insalata sorbetto agnello zuppa torta zucchini

primi piatti	secondi piatti	contorni	dolci

3   How would you say you like the following?

a il prosciutto   b le tagliatelle al ragù
c il risotto alla marinara   d il vitello ai funghi
e la torta di mele   f le fragole

How would you say you don't like them?

4   Supply the final vowel to the adjectives in these sentences.
Ottimo and **squisito** are often used to describe something which is excellent.

a Questo vino è ottim_.
b Gli spaghetti sono buonissim_.
c Complimenti per una cena squisit_.
d Le fragole sono molto buon_.
e Questa torta è delizios_.

now you're talking!

1   **2•79** Imagine you're going for a meal in the Trattoria Chiezzi with a partner who doesn't speak Italian. You might need the menu from page 88.

You're greeted by Emilio ...
- **Buongiorno, signori. Tavolo per due?**
- ◆ Say yes, for two.
- **Ecco il menù.**
- ◆ Thank him.

He returns a few minutes later.
- **Pronti per ordinare?**
- ◆ Ask for seafood risotto and cannelloni.
- **E per secondo?**
- ◆ Ask what he recommends.
- **Il pesce è buono oggi – molto buono.**
- ◆ Order the fish and the chicken in garlic.
- **E come contorno?**
- ◆ Order potatoes and courgettes.

When he brings the food ...
- **Ecco ... pesce ... e pollo. Buon appetito.**
- ◆ Say you'd like a carafe of red wine.
- **Un litro?**
- ◆ Say half a litre.

He comes back when you have finished.
- **Tutto bene? Le piace il pesce?**
- ◆ Say yes, you like it, it's very good.
- **Dessert, signori?**
- ◆ Ask what the **torta della casa** is.
- **È una torta di pere con panna. Le piacciono le pere?**
- ◆ Say you like them a lot but you don't like cream.
- ◆ Order ice cream and cheese.
- **Va bene.**

quiz

1 How would you ask for a table for two?

2 What is the main ingredient of a dish **all'aglio**?

3 To say you like **lasagne al forno** would you use **mi piace** or **mi piacciono**?

4 How do you say you don't want a pudding?

5 What do you say to attract the waiter's attention?

6 Is lamb **vitello** or **agnello**?

7 What is *very good indeed* when describing **il tiramisù**?

8 Which one of these is not a **contorno**?
spinaci, insalata, maiale, zucchini

9 How do you ask if you can taste the cheese?

10 Before starting your meal, what would you say to the people eating with you?

Now check whether you can ...

- understand the main points of an Italian menu
- ask about items on the menu
- order a meal with drinks
- say what you like and what you don't like
- ask others what they like
- pay a compliment

Bravo! You have reached the end of **Talk Italian**.

And now ... prepare yourself for the **Controllo finale** *final checkpoint* with some revision. Listen to the conversations again – the more you listen the more confident you will become. You can test your knowledge of the key phrases by covering up the English on the lists. Look back at the final pages of each unit and use the quizzes and checklists to assess how much you remember. Take every opportunity to speak Italian; if no one else is available, talk aloud to yourself!

Controllo finale

Imagine you have just arrived in Italy on holiday ...

1   It's Sunday. You arrive at Santa Maria Novella station in Florence,
    tired and thirsty, and look for a bar. Which of these questions would
    you ask?

    a   **Scusi, dov'è il duomo?**
    b   **Scusi, c'è un albergo qui?**
    c   **Scusi, c'è un bar qui vicino?**

2   **2•80** Having found one, you go to the **cassa**. Now listen to the audio
    and be ready to order a drink.

    You ....
    Cassiera **Un euro e ottantadue. Ecco lo scontrino.**
    You ....

    a   How much change should you expect from a 10 euro note?
    b   What is a **scontrino**?

3   **2•81** After your drink, how would you ask the barman ...

    a   if you can make a phone call from here?
    b   where the toilet is?
    c   if the tourist office is open today?   **Scusi, signore!**
    d   how much the postcards cost?

4   You then ask him where the Hotel Arcangelo is. Listen and make a
    note in English of the directions he gives you.

    ....
    ....
    ....

5 Before finding the hotel, you go back to the station to find out when the first train leaves for Rome on Tuesday morning, what time it arrives and how much a single ticket costs.
For each question, choose the correct option.

  a **A che ora parte il <u>primo</u>/<u>prossimo</u> treno per Roma <u>martedì</u>/<u>mercoledì</u>?**
  b **A che ora arriva <u>da</u>/<u>a</u> Roma?**
  c **Quanto <u>costa</u>/<u>costano</u> un biglietto <u>di andata e ritorno</u>/<u>di andata</u>?**

6 At the Arcangelo you have already booked a single room with shower until Tuesday. At reception, after saying who you are, which of the following would you say?

  a **Vorrei una camera singola con bagno fino a giovedì.**
  b **Ho prenotato una camera singola senza bagno fino a martedì.**
  c **Avete una camera a due letti fino a mercoledì?**
  d **Ho prenotato una camera singola con doccia fino a martedì.**

7 2•82 Listen to the receptionist's reply. Make a note in English of the two things she asks you, and also of your room number and which floor it's on.

  a ....
  b ....
  c **Camera** ....   **Piano** ....

8 2•83 The Hotel Arcangelo will change money for you. Listen to the manager telling you the rate of exchange (**il cambio**) for the pound (**sterlina**). What does he say is the current rate?

  a € 1,56
  b € 1,66
  c € 1,86

9 2•84 That evening in the hotel bar, you start chatting to Paul Durand who is French from **Nizza** *Nice*. He's in marketing and travels a lot. Listen to his plans for the week and note where he is going in the diary. **Vado** means *I'm going*.

Mon		Fri	
Tues		Sat	
Wed		Sun	
Thur			

10 Can you now work out how Paul would answer these three questions?

   a **Come si chiama?**

   b **È italiano?**

   c **Dove abita?**

What questions would you need to ask him if these are his answers?

   d ....

     Sì, sono sposato.

   e ....

     Si chiama Christiane.

   f ....

     Sì, ho una figlia – Amélie.

   g ....

     Ha sei anni.

   h ....

     Sono direttore del marketing.

   i ....

     Sì, parlo inglese ... e anche italiano, tedesco e giapponese.

   j ....

     No, non mi piace lo sport.

   2•85 Now it's your turn to answer some questions. Listen to the audio.

11 Paul is planning to bring his family to Italy on a camping holiday and shows you information about Campeggio La Pineta.

	alta stagione luglio/agosto	**bassa stagione** aprile – giugno settembre/ottobre
★★★★ Campeggio La Pineta Tel: 059/22339		
piazzola	€ 21	€ 17
adulto	€ 15	€ 10
bambino (2 – 12)	€ 6,50	€ 4,50

Prices are per night. Can you work out the price for Paul and his family to stay in La Pineta for six nights in July? **Una piazzola** is a place in a campsite. If he pays by cheque, how will he write the amount in words?

12 The two of you decide not to eat in the hotel but to try this restaurant Paul has seen advertised.

> ristorante
> # AL VIGNETO
>
> specialità carne e pesce alla griglia
> cucina casareccia tradizionale • vini locali
> posizione panoramica con giardino
>
> chiuso il lunedì da novembre a aprile

a What is the house speciality?
b Is the restaurant closed tonight (Sunday)?
c What kind of wines can you expect?
d What is special about **cucina casareccia**?

Transcripts and answers

This section contains scripts of all the conversations. Answers which consist of words from the conversations are given in bold type in the scripts.

Unit 1

Pages 8 & 9

2 • Buongiorno, **signore**. *(m)*
   ◆ Buongiorno, signora.
   ◆ Ah, **signora Riccardi** – buongiorno.
   ◆ Come sta?
   ● Bene grazie.
   ◆ Buongiorno!
   ● Buongiorno, **signor Chiesa**.
   The first person is a man.

3 • **Buona sera.**
   ◆ Buona sera, signor Conti.
   ● Buona sera, signora. Come sta?
   ◆ Bene, grazie. E lei?
   ● Bene, grazie.

4 • **Ciao**, Carla, **buongiorno**.
   ◆ **Ciao**, Giorgio.
   ● **Ciao!** Come stai?
   ◆ Bene, grazie.
   ● **Ciao, buongiorno.**

6 • Arrivederci, Claudia, **buongiorno**.
   ● Arrivederci, signor Chiesa.
   ● Arrivederci, signora.
   ● Arrivederci, signor Conti.

7 • **Ciao**, Angela. **Arrivederci.**
   ● **Ciao**, Francesca. **Buongiorno.**

8 • Buona notte, **signore**. *(m)*
   ● Buona notte, **signora**. *(f)*
   ● Buona notte, **signora Ricci**. *(f)*
   ● Buona notte, **signor Conti**. *(m)*
   Two men and two women.

9 • Buongiorno, signor Calvi.
   ● Ciao, Carlo, buona sera.
   ● Buona sera, signore.
   ● Buona sera, signora.
   ● Ciao, Lucia.

10 • Come sta, signor Calvi?
   ● Come stai, Carlo?

● Arrivederci, signor Calvi.

Pages 10 & 11

2 • Buongiorno, signora.
   Sono **Enrico Piacenza**.
   ● Buongiorno. Sono **Giovanna Ricci**.
   ● Signora Ricci … buongiorno.
   ● Io sono **Roberto Riccardi**.
   Roberto (not Paolo) Riccardi.

3 • Buongiorno, signore. Signore, **lei è?**
   ◆ Mancini. Sono Luciano Mancini.

5 • **Mi chiamo** Francesca Como. **Come si chiama?**
   ◆ Luciano, Luciano Mancini. **Piacere.**
   ● **Piacere.**

6 • Buona sera, signora. Enrico Piacenza.
   ◆ Piacere. Io mi chiamo Giovanna Ricci.
   ● **Scusi?**
   ◆ Ricci – Giovanna Ricci.
   ● Piacere.

7 • Buongiorno. Come si **chiama**?
   ◆ **Mi** chiamo Franco Lelli.
   ● Ciao. **Come** ti chiami?
   ◆ **Mi** chiamo Giulia.
   ● E tu, come ti chiami?
   ◆ Mi **chiamo** Marcella.

8 • Ciao **Gemma**. Ciao **Guido**.
   ◆ **Giovanna!** Ciao! Come stai?
   ● Buona sera. Come stai?
   ◆ Bene, bene … questo è **Geraldo**.

Page 12

1 *a* Buona notte; *b* Ciao; *c* Mi chiamo;
   d Io sono; *e* Buongiorno;
   f Come sta?; *g* Arrivederci;
   h Buona sera; *i* Come si chiama?;
   j Piacere.

2 *a* Buongiorno, signora. –
   Buongiorno, signore.
   b Buona sera. – Ciao, buona sera.

c Ciao, come stai? – Bene.
d Buona notte. – Buona notte.

Page 13

1 ● Buongiorno. Come sta?
  ◆ **Bene grazie, e lei?**
  ● Bene, grazie.
  ◆ **Buongiorno, signora. Sono
  + *your name.***
  ● Piacere. Io sono Anna Alberti.
  ◆ **Scusi?**
  ● Anna Alberti.
  ◆ **Piacere.**

  ◆ **Buongiorno. Lei è Luciano
  Mironi?**
  ● No, sono Luciano Mancini.
  ◆ **Io sono + *your name*. Piacere.**
  ● Piacere.
  ◆ **Arrivederci, Anna, arrivederci
  Luciano.**
  ● Arrivederci.

2 ● **Buona sera, signora.**
  ◆ Buona sera. Come sta?
  ● **Bene, grazie ... Ciao!**
  ◆ Buona sera.
  ● **Come ti chiami?**
  ◆ Mi chiamo Giulia.
  ● **E come stai, Giulia?**
  ◆ Bene, grazie.
  ● **Arrivederci, buona sera.**

Page 14

1 to say hello or goodbye informally;
2 Piacere; *3* late afternoon and
evening; *4* lei; *5* before a surname;
6 Bene, grazie – e lei? *7* to wish
someone good night; *8* io sono/
mi chiamo; *9* Moschino; *10* Come ti
chiami?

Unit 2

Pages 16 & 17

2 ● Signora, lei è inglese?
  ◆ Sì, sono **inglese.**
  ● Lei è inglese?
  ◆ No. Io sono **americano.**
  Sono di Chicago.

● Buongiorno, signore.
  Lei è americano?
◆ No, io non sono americano,
  sono **inglese.**
● E lei, signora? È inglese o
  americana?
◆ Sono **australiana!**
● Di dov'è?
● Sono di Perth.

3 ● Come ti chiami?
  ◆ Fiorella.
  ● Sei italiana, no?
  ◆ Sì.
  ● **Di dove sei?**
  ◆ Di **Bergamo.**

4 Italia – **italiano;** Inghilterra –
  inglese; Scozia – **scozzese;** Irlanda
  – **irlandese;** Galles – **gallese;** Stati
  Uniti – **americano;** Australia –
  australiano; Svizzera – **svizzero;**
  Francia – **francese;** Germania –
  tedesco; Spagna – **spagnolo;** Canada
  – **canadese**

6 ● Antonio è **spagnolo,** di Madrid.
  ● Helen è **americana.**
  ● Mike è di Toronto, è **canadese.**
  ● Anna è **scozzese.** È di Edimburgo.

Page 18

2 ● Signore, che lavoro fa?
  ◆ Sono **giornalista.**
  ● Che lavoro fa?
  ◆ Sono **ingegnere.**
  ● Signora, che lavoro fa?
  ◆ Sono **segretaria.**

3 ● Che lavoro fa?
  ◆ Sono **guida.**
  ● Tu sei studente?
  ◆ No, non sono studente.
  ● Che lavoro fai?
  ◆ Sono **ragioniere.**
  ● Lei è artista?
  ◆ Sì, ma sono **disoccupato.**
  ma = *but*

Page 19

4 ● Buongiorno, signore.

- Che lavoro fa lei?
- Sono **professore d'italiano** (teacher of Italian).
- Lei è italiano, vero?
- No, non sono italiano – sono **scozzese** (Scottish).

2 • Qual è il tuo numero di telefono, Gemma?
- **zero, sette, nove, due, sette, zero, cinque, uno, nove.**
- Paolo?
- **zero, cinque, nove, due, uno, sette, otto, quattro, tre.**

Gemma 079 270519;
Paolo 059 217843

Page 20

1 *a* No, sono americana;
b No, non sono italiano; *c* Sono di Milano; *d* No, io sono romano;
e Sono infermiera.

2 Cognome: Manuzzi   Nome: Marco
Nazionalità: Italiano
Professione: Medico

3 • Mi **chiamo** Ulrike Schmitt. Sono **tedesca**, di Berlino e sono **dentista**.
- Mi chiamo Angela Roberts. Sono gallese, di Bangor, e sono segretaria.
- Mi chiamo Marco Blondini. Sono italiano, di Roma, e sono ragioniere.

Page 21

1 • Scusi, dov'è il Municipio?
- **Non sono di qui.**
- Lei non è italiana?
- **No, sono inglese.**
- Di dov'è?
- **Sono di Chester. Di dov'è lei?**
- Sono veneziano.
- **Scusi?**
- Sono di Venezia – sono veneziano.

2 • Signor Fairlie, lei è inglese?
- **No, non sono inglese, sono scozzese.**
- Di dov'è?
- **Sono di Edimburgo.**

- Che lavoro fa?
- **Sono architetto.**

3 • Buongiorno! Come sta?
- **Bene, grazie.**
- Sono Pietro. Lei, come si chiama?
- **Mi chiamo +** *your name.*
- Lei è americano?
- **Sono +** *your nationality.*
- Di dov'è?
- **Sono di +** *your home town.*
- Che lavoro fa?
- **Sono +** *your job.*

Page 22

1 Sono italiana; 2 Sono di Chester;
3 quattro, otto; 4 Di dov'è?;
5 Di dove sei?; 6 Non sono di qui;
7 impiegato; 8 Florence; 9 Non;
10 autrice

Unit 3

Pages 24 & 25

2 • Buongiorno, signora Cesare. **Questo** è Paolo Lega.
- Piacere.
- E **questa** è Camilla Faldi.
- Piacere.

4 • Mario – questo è mio marito **Piero**.
- Piacere.
- Questa è **Marta**, mia moglie.
- Piacere, Marta.

5 • Sei sposata, Alessandra?
- Sono divorziata.
- Tu sei sposato, Ettore?
- Sì, sono sposato. E tu Mario, sei sposato tu?
- Io? No, non sono sposato. Sono single.

Mario è single; Alessandra è divorziata;
Ettore è sposato.

7 • Hai bambini, Camilla?
- Sì, ho **un figlio** e **una figlia**.
- E tu, Marta, hai bambini?
- Ho **un figlio**. Roberto! Questo è **mio figlio**.

8 • Renata, hai figli tu?

◆ Io? No, non sono sposata.
She's not married and has no children.

9 ● Questo è Enrico Piacenza.
  ● Questa è Francesca.
  ● Questo è mio marito …/
    Questa è mia moglie …

Pages 26 & 27

2 Quattordici (14).

3 quindici, cinquantacinque,
  dodici, quarantasei, ottantasette,
  settantatré.

5 ● Ciao. Sono Laura. Questa è
    Marianna. Tu, come ti chiami?
  ● Massimo.
  ● Quanti anni hai?
  ◆ **Diciassette** – e tu?
  ● **Diciassette** anch'io.
  ◆ Quanti anni hai, Marianna?
  ● **Sedici.**
  Massimo is 17; Laura is 17;
  Marianna is 16.

6 ● Lei ha figli?
  ◆ Ho una **figlia**, Caterina, e ho anche
    un **figlio**.
  ● Come si **chiama**?
  ◆ Stefano.
  ● E quanti anni **ha**?
  ◆ Ha **undici** (11) anni.

7 ● Mi chiamo Anna. Sono sposata e
    questo è Vittorio, mio marito.
    Questa è mia figlia Sofia. (c)
  ● Sono Alessandra Rossi. Io sono
    divorziata. Questa è mia figlia
    Caterina e questo è Stefano, mio
    figlio. (a)
  ● Mi chiamo Lorenzo. Non sono
    sposato. Questo è mio padre e
    questa è mia sorella Gianna. (b)

Page 28

1 *a* Mio padre si chiama Roberto; *b* Mia
  sorella si chiama Caterina; *c* Isabella
  è mia figlia; *d* Isabella ha 13 anni;
  e vero; *f* vero; *g* falso

2 gemelli – *twins*

Page 29

1 ● Buongiorno, signora. Come si
    chiama?
  ◆ **Mi chiamo Anna Fraser.**
  ● Lei è sposata?
  ◆ **Sì, questo è mio marito Jonathan.**
  ● Ha figli?
  ◆ **Ho una figlia e un figlio.**
  ● Come si chiama sua figlia?
  ◆ **Si chiama Sarah.**
  ● Quanti anni ha?
  ◆ **Quattordici.**
  ● E suo figlio – come si chiama?
  ◆ **Si chiama Daniel.**
  ● Quanti anni ha?
  ◆ **Ha dodici anni.**

2 ● Tu sei sposato?
  ◆ **Sì, sono sposato/a./No, non sono**
    sposato/a. E tu, sei sposato?
  ● Sì, mia moglie si chiama Caterina.
  ◆ **Hai figli?**
  ● Sì – una figlia.
  ◆ **Come si chiama?**
  ● Laura.
  ◆ **Quanti anni ha?**
  ● Ha otto anni.
  ◆ **Questo/a è +** *friend/partner's*
    name.
  ● Piacere.

Page 30

1 questa è; *2* Anna, questo è mio
fratello; *3* mia figlia; *4* sorella;
5 my father; *6* quanti anni hai?
7 ho … anni; *8* 15; *9* novantanove 99

Unit 4
Pages 32 & 33

2 ● Mi dica.
  ◆ **Una birra**, per favore.
  ● Una birra, signore. Va bene.

3 ● Buongiorno. Prego?
  ◆ **Un caffè**, per favore.
  ● Una coca.
  ◆ **Un caffè e una coca.**

- Un gelato, per favore.
- Un'aranciata per me.
- Un caffè, una coca, un gelato e un'aranciata … va bene …

madre – caffè; padre – coca; figlia – gelato; figlio – aranciata

4
- Prego?
- **Un caffè**, per favore.
- Caffè **anche per me**.
- Con zucchero, Daniela?
- No, no, grazie – **senza** zucchero.

5
- Buona sera.
- Signora, buona sera. Mi dica.
- Un'acqua minerale, per favore.
- Gassata o non gassata?
- **Non gassata**. E un **cappuccino** per mia figlia.
- Allora, un **cappuccino** e un'acqua minerale **non gassata**. Va bene.

6
- Mi dica, signora.
- Un cappuccino, per favore.
- Signore?
- Un bicchiere di acqua minerale.
- Gassata o non gassata?
- Gassata.
- Zucchero, Anna?
- Sì, grazie.

a falso; b vero; c vero; d falso

7 una birra, per favore; un caffè, per favore; un gelato, per favore

Pages 34 & 35

2
- Buongiorno, Mario.
- Ah, buongiorno, signor Guarino. Come sta?
- Bene, bene.
- Prende un caffè?
- **Sì, grazie.**
- Due caffè, per favore.
- Subito, signore.
- Luisa – buongiorno … un caffè?
- Sì, grazie – **un caffè macchiato**.

3
- Che cosa prendi, Claudia?
- Una birra.
- E tu, Fabio?
- Una birra anche per me.
- Allora, **tre birre**, per favore.

- Grazie.
- Prego.

They all order beer.

4
- Anita, che cosa prende?
- Un bicchiere di vino.
- Rosso o bianco?
- **Rosso**.
- Per lei, signora?
- Un bicchiere di **rosso** anche per me.
- Un bicchiere di vino **bianco** e due bicchieri di vino rosso.

Antonio – vino bianco; Anita and signora Perrone – vino rosso

5
- Signor Howard, che cosa prende?
- Come si dice in italiano 'whisky'?
- Whisky!
- Allora, **un whisky**.
- **Con ghiaccio?**
- **Sì**, grazie.
- Signor Guarino, prende **un whisky** anche lei?
- Volentieri.
- **Con ghiaccio?**
- **No – senza.**
- Allora, due whisky – uno con ghiaccio e uno senza – e **un Martini rosso**.
- Cin cin! Cin cin!

Signor Howard – con ghiaccio; Signor Guarino – senza ghiaccio; Mario – Martini rosso

Page 36

1 un caffè; un cappuccino; un tè; un'acqua minerale; un vino; una spremuta; una birra; una grappa; un gelato; un frullato; un'aranciata; un amaro

2
- Buongiorno, Antonia – prende un caffè?
- Volentieri – senza zucchero, per favore.
- E tu, Fabrizio – prendi un bicchiere di vino?
- No grazie – un caffè anche per me.

- Allora due caffè e un bicchiere di vino bianco per me.

3 *a* Due birre e un cappuccino.
   b Due cappuccini e un caffè.
   c Due caffè e un bicchiere di vino.
   d Due aranciate e un gelato.

Page 37

1 ● **Che cosa prendi, Emilio?**
   ◆ Un bicchiere di vino bianco.
   ● **Che cosa prendi, Francesca?**
   ◆ Un'aranciata, per favore.
   ● **Buongiorno, signora. Un bicchiere di vino bianco, un'aranciata e una birra, per favore.**

2 ● Prende un caffè?
   ◆ **Volentieri. Un cappuccino, per favore.**
   ● Con zucchero?
   ◆ **Senza zucchero.**

3 ● **Come si dice in italiano 'milk shake'?**

4 ● Buongiorno. Prego?
   ◆ **Due bicchieri di vino e due birre.**
   ● Vino bianco o rosso?
   ◆ **Rosso.**
   ● **Grazie – cin cin!**

Page 38

1 zucchero; *2* caffè corretto;
3 con ghiaccio; *4* vini, birre, bicchieri;
5 a receipt; *6* masculine; *7* cin cin;
8 sparkling; *9* Sì, grazie, Volentieri;
10 Prego.

Punto di controllo 1
Pages 39–42

1 ● Buongiorno, signora. Lei è qui in vacanza o per lavoro?
   ◆ **In vacanza.**
   ● Come si chiama?
   ◆ Laura Santoro.
   ● È italiana?
   ◆ No, non sono italiana, sono **americana**. Però, mio **padre è italiano** e io sono **in Italia con mia nonna.**
   ● Di dov'è?
   ◆ Sono **di San Diego.**
   ● È sposata?
   ◆ Sono **divorziata.**
   ● Ha bambini?
   ◆ Sì, ho **un figlio.**
   ● E che lavoro fa?
   ◆ Sono **disoccupata.**
   ● Grazie, signora. Arrivederci e buongiorno.

2 ● Ciao. Come ti chiami?
   ◆ Caterina.
   ● Piacere. Io sono Jonathan.
   ◆ Tu non sei italiano, vero?
   ● **Sono irlandese.** Tu sei **italiana?**
   ◆ Sì. Sei in vacanza?
   ● No. Sono studente qui – a Perugia.
   ◆ Quanti anni hai?
   ● **Diciotto.** Quanti anni hai tu?
   ◆ **Diciannove.** Hai fratelli?
   ● Ho **due sorelle e un fratello.** E tu?
   ◆ Ho **una sorella.**
   Caterina – Italian, 19, one sister.
   Jonathan – Irish, 18, two sisters and a brother.

3 ● Che cosa prendi?
   ◆ Acqua minerale – gassata.
   ◆ Per favore – **un bicchiere di acqua minerale gassata** e **una birra.**
   ◆ Cin cin.
   ● Allora, arrivederci … Ecco il mio numero di telefono a Perugia: **zero, sette, cinque, sette, quattro, tre, zero, zero.**
   ◆ Il mio numero è **zero, sei, uno, otto, due, quattro, cinque, sei.**
   ● Arrivederci.
   Caterina – sparkling mineral water, 0618 2456; Jonathan – beer, 075 74300.

5 Danimarca *(Denmark)* 19; Grecia *(Greece)* 75; Irlanda *(Ireland)* **99**; Israele *(Israel)* **47**; Lussemburgo *(Luxembury)* **72**; Norvegia *(Norway)*

12; Olanda (Holland) **70**; Portogallo (Portugal) **83**

6 *a* Sì, grazie; *b* Prego; *c* Scusi?
d Piacere; *e* Bene, grazie; *f* Cin cin.

7 *a* Come si chiama?/Come ti chiami?
b Quanti anni ha/hai?
c Che lavoro fa/fai?

8 birra, questo, lavoro, nonna, inglese, quanti, vino, prende, con, come
BUONGIORNO

9 Dear Rachel, my name's Alessandra Giardi and I'm Sicilian, from Siracusa. I'm 14. There are five of us in the family – my father Massimo who is unemployed, my mother Giuseppina who is a nurse at the hospital and my brother Stefano who is a student. Stefano is 19. There's also my grandmother …

Unit 5

Pages 44 & 45

2 ● Allora Mario, **la stazione è qui**.
   ◆ Dov'è **il duomo**?
   ● **E lì**.
   ◆ E **la questura**, dov'è?
   ● **È dietro il municipio**.
   ◆ Dov'è **l'azienda di turismo**?
   ● **In centro città** – qui.
   ◆ E **dov'è l'ufficio postale**?
   ● … **è in via della Vittoria**.
   ◆ È lontano?
   ● Sì … No … dieci minuti a piedi.
   La stazione è qui; Il duomo è lì;
   L'azienda di turismo è in centro città;
   La questura è dietro il municipio;
   L'ufficio postale è in via della Vittoria.

4 ● Scusi, signore, dov'è il Municipio?
   ◆ È in Piazza Garibaldi, in centro.
   ● Può ripetere, per favore?
   ◆ È in Piazza Garibaldi … non è qui, è in centro …
   ● Grazie. Può parlare lentamente?
   ◆ **È in centro, lontano da qui … venti minuti a piedi.**

It's in the centre, a long way away, twenty minutes' walk.

5 ● Scusi, **dove sono** i negozi?
   ◆ Sono lì, **in centro**.
   ● È lontano il centro?
   ◆ No, no – a **500 metri, cinque minuti a piedi**.
   ● Può ripetere per favore?
   ◆ Cinque minuti a piedi – 500 metri.
   In the centre, 500 m away; 5 minutes.

6 Dov'è l'azienda di turismo/l'ufficio turistico?
Dov'è l'ufficio postale?
Dov'è la stazione?
Dove sono i negozi?

Pages 46 & 47

2 ● Signora, abita qui a Bologna?
   ◆ Abito **in periferia**.
   ● Abita qui a Bologna, signore?
   ◆ Sì – abito qui **in centro città**.
   ● Scusi signora, dove abita?
   ◆ Lontano da qui – **in campagna**.
   sig.ra 1 – in periferia; sig. – in centro;
   sig.ra 2 – in campagna.

3/4
   ● Signora Bonino, dove abita?
   ◆ Io abito qui a Bologna, in una casa, viale Roma **34**.
   ● E lei, signor Quarta, abita qui?
   ◆ Sì, in un appartamento. Piazza Garibaldi, numero **6**.
   ● Signora Galli, anche lei abita in un appartamento?
   ◆ Sì, ho un appartamento in un palazzo in via Verdi **27**. E mia figlia abita in una villetta in via Aurelia **53**.
   sig.ra Bonino – viale Roma 34; sig.
   Quarta – piazza Garibaldi 6; sig.ra Galli
   – via Verdi 27; la figlia di Caterina – via
   Aurelia 53.

7 ● **Signora Galli**, dove lavora?
   ◆ Lavoro nella zona industriale – **per la Zanussi**.
   ● E tu, **Luciano**, dove lavori?

◆ Lavoro **in un ufficio** in centro.
● E tu, Franca?
◆ Io non lavoro.
Signora Galli works for Zanussi.
Luciano works in an office.

8 ● Scusi, dove lavora?
◆ Per la Fiat. *(1)*
● Dove lavora lei?
◆ In una pizzeria in centro. *(2)*
● E lei, dove lavora?
◆ Lavoro in un ufficio in via
   Puccini. *(3)*
● Scusi, signora, dove lavora?
◆ A Roma – abito e lavoro a
   Roma. *(4)*
● Dove lavori?
◆ Non lavoro – sono studente. *(5)*
He's a student.

Page 48

1 *a* il, i, la; *b* la, l', l'; *c* il, l', la; *d* la, il, i

2 *a* È in centro; *b* Lavoro in via Marconi;
   c Sì, abito qui; *d* Sono in centro;
   e No, lavoro in centro; *f* Cinque
   minuti a piedi.

3 *a* **a** Firenze; *b* **in** piazza Garibaldi; *c*
   a Milano; *d* **in** via Manzini; *e* **in** un
   negozio; *f* **in** una pizzeria; *g* **in** un
   ufficio; *h* **a** Roma.
   (**a** with towns; **in** with buildings,
   streets and squares, countries, islands)

4 appartamento, duecento, municipio,
   gli, periferia

Page 49

1 ● **Buongiorno, signora, dov'è il**
     Duomo?
   ◆ Il Duomo? È in centro – in Piazza
     Duomo.
   ● **È lontano?**
   ◆ No, no, dieci minuti a piedi.
   ● **E dov'è il municipio?**
   ◆ È dietro il Duomo.
   ● **Scusi? Può ripetere, per favore?**

2 ● **Dove sono i negozi?**
   ◆ Sono in via Michelangelo, a due
     passi.

● **Può parlare più lentamente?**
◆ In via Michelangelo, a due passi …
   non è lontano.
● **Grazie signore.**

3 ● Lei è tedesco?
   ◆ **No, sono +** *your nationality.*
   ● Dove abita?
   ◆ **Abito a +** *your town.*
   ● Abita in centro città?
   ◆ **No, abito +** *where you live.*
   ● E dove lavora?
   ◆ e.g. **Lavoro a Londra, per la BBC.**

4 ● **Abita qui?**
   ◆ No, lavoro qui ma abito in via
     Belloni.
   ● **Dov'è via Belloni?**
   ◆ Non è lontano – è in periferia, a
     quindici minuti da qui.

Page 50

1 qui; 2 dov'è? – where is?, dove sono?
– where are? 3 behind the station;
4 abita in periferia; 5 la birra, il figlio,
l'Italia; 6 the old part of town;
7 quattrocento; 8 non; 9 Where do you
live? Where does he/she live?;
10 trecentocinquanta

Unit 6

Pages 52 & 53

2 banca *bank*; albergo *hotel*; mercato
market; museo *museum*; stazione
station; piscina *swimming pool*;
supermercato *supermarket*; farmacia
chemist's; ristorante *restaurant*;
teatro *theatre*.

3 ● Ecco l'azienda di promozione
     turistica qui. In città c'è un **teatro**
     e un **museo**. C'è il **mercato**
     in centro e ci sono anche tre
     supermercati. Ci sono **trattorie** e
     molti **ristoranti**.
   ◆ Dov'è la **piscina**?
   ● Non c'è una piscina qui, ma ce
     n'è una a Forlini, a 15 chilometri
     da qui.

- Dov'è la **stazione**?
- La stazione è in centro – non è lontano da qui. Ecco una piantina, signore.

4 *a* falso; *b* vero; *c* vero; *d* vero

6 • La piscina è aperta **ogni giorno**. **Lunedì** e **venerdì** c'è un mercato in Piazza Marconi in centro. Il museo è chiuso **oggi**; è aperto **martedì**, **giovedì** e **sabato**. L'azienda di turismo è chiusa **domenica**.

Pages 54 & 55

2 • Scusi, c'è un telefono qui?
- ◆ Ecco **qui a sinistra**.
- Grazie. C'è una toilette?
- ◆ **Lì in fondo a destra**, signora.

3 • Scusi, signore, c'è una banca qui vicino?
- ◆ Mi dispiace, **non lo so** – non sono di qui.

4 • Scusi, signore, c'è una banca qui vicino?
- ◆ Sì, in via Mazzini – **a destra** e poi a sinistra.
- A destra poi a sinistra. Grazie.
Right and then left.

5 • Scusi, signore, c'è una farmacia qui vicino?
- Giorgio, c'è una farmacia qui vicino?
- Ce n'è una in via Vittorio Emanuele – **a sinistra, la prima a destra poi sempre dritto**.
- ◆ Può ripetere, per favore?
- A sinistra, la prima a destra poi sempre dritto.
Left, first right, straight on.

6 • Scusi, signora, dov'è l'azienda di turismo?
- ◆ **In Corso Italia – in centro.** È lontano da qui.
- È aperta oggi?
- ◆ **Non lo so**, mi dispiace.
- C'è un autobus?

- ◆ Sì – c'è il **sedici**.
- Grazie.
We don't know if it's open. Bus no. 16.

7 • Scusi, signore, dov'è l'azienda di turismo?
- ◆ Sempre dritto fino al semaforo – **cinquecento metri** – poi **a destra**.
500 m; right at lights.

8 • Buongiorno. C'è un mercato qui?
- ◆ Sì c'è un mercato martedì e venerdì in Piazza Italia.
- C'è un museo?
- ◆ Ci sono due musei; tutti e due sono chiusi domenica.
- C'è una piscina?
- ◆ Sì, in via Garibaldi.
- È aperta oggi?
- ◆ È aperta ogni giorno, signora.
- Ci sono magazzini?
- ◆ Sì, in centro. Sono aperti da lunedì a sabato, e chiusi domenica.
- Grazie. Arrivederci.

a falso; *b* vero; *c* vero; *d* vero; *e* vero; *f* falso

9 • C'è una banca qui vicino?
- C'è una farmacia qui vicino?
- C'è un ristorante qui vicino?
- C'è un supermercato qui vicino?

Page 56

1 *a* Monday; *b* Yes, mornings only; *c* every day; *d* Tuesday

Page 57

1 • **Scusi, signore, c'è una farmacia qui vicino?**
- ◆ Una farmacia … Sì, a sinistra poi sempre dritto.
- **A sinistra, poi sempre dritto. Grazie.**

2 • **Scusi, c'è un supermercato qui vicino?**
- ◆ C'è l'ipermercato a Molinella … ma è lontano.
- **C'è un autobus?**
- ◆ Sì, deve prendere il numero quarantadue.

- Il quarantadue. Grazie signora. Arrivederci.

3
- C'è un bar qui vicino?
- Lì a sinistra – ecco.
- Grazie; c'è un albergo qui vicino?
- Mi dispiace, non lo so.
- Dov'è l'azienda di turismo?
- A destra, sempre dritto duecento metri, poi la prima a sinistra.
- A destra, sempre dritto duecento metri, poi la prima a sinistra. È aperta?
- Sì, sì.

4
- Ci sono ristoranti qui vicino?
- In via Doria c'è la Trattoria Corallo.
- È lontano?
- No, no, cinque minuti a piedi.

Page 58

1 Tourist information office; *2* right;
3 ristorante, trattoria, pizzeria;
4 C'è un telefono? *5* closed; *6* c'è;
7 sabato (Sat) and domenica (Sun);
8 a map; *9* non lo so; *10* magazzini

Unit 7
Pages 60 & 61

2 *a* € 13 *b* € 0,75 *c* € 24,99 *d* € 82
e € 12,25 *f* € 350

4 una guida di Firenze *guidebook of Florence*; tre cartoline *postcards*; un giornale inglese *English newspaper*; tre francobolli *stamps*; una carta telefonica *telephone card*; cerotti *plasters*.

5
- Buongiorno. Dica.
- Signora, quanto **costa** questa guida?
- **Dieci** euro (€ 10).
- E quanto **costano** i giornali inglesi?
- **Un euro e quindici** (€ 1,15).

6
- Buongiorno, mi dica.
- **Quanto costano i cerotti?**
- Cerotti … questi costano € 2,49.

7
- Scusi, quanto costano le cartoline?

- Trenta centesimi.
- Quanto costa un francobollo per la Gran Bretagna?
- Quarantuno.
- E un francobollo per gli Stati Uniti?
- Cinquantadue centesimi.
- Avete carte telefoniche?
- Mi dispiace, no.

cartolina € 0,30; francobollo per la Gran Bretagna € 0,41; francobollo per gli Stati Uniti € 0,52.

8
- Buongiorno. Dica.
- Avete biglietti per l'autobus?
- Sì, certo.
- Quanto costano?
- Un euro e dieci il biglietto.
- Mi dà quattro, no cinque biglietti.
- Cinque e cinquanta, signore.
- Grazie. Quattro euro e cinquanta di resto. Arrivederci, signore.

One ticket – € 1,10; he buys five tickets; change € 4,50.

9 Avete francobolli? Avete una guida? Avete biglietti per l'autobus? Quanto costa una cartolina? Quanto costano i biglietti per l'autobus? Quanto costa un giornale inglese?

Pages 62 & 63

1 Allora … sei panini, mezzo chilo di formaggio, un etto di prosciutto, mezzo litro di olio di oliva, un litro di acqua minerale, una bottiglia di vino rosso e **una bottiglia di vino bianco** e un chilo di zucchero.

3
- Buongiorno, signora. Mi dica.
- Mi dà un litro di acqua minerale.
- Gassata o non gassata?
- Gassata … e due bottiglie di vino, bianco e rosso.
- Acqua minerale, gassata, due bottiglie di vino. Altro?
- Mezzo chilo di formaggio … un etto di prosciutto … e quanto costa l'olio di oliva extra vergine?
- € 7,50 il litro, € 4,00 mezzo litro.
- Ne prendo mezzo litro.

- Basta così?
◆ No – mi dà sei panini … e basta.
- 28 euro e 20, signora.
Still to buy: a kilo of sugar.

4 - Buongiorno. Vorrei un **chilo di mele** e un chilo di banane.
◆ … Altro?
- Mi dà **mezzo chilo di pomodori** e **250 grammi di funghi**.
◆ Mezzo chilo di pomodori e 250 grammi di funghi. Basta così?
- Quanto costano le fragole?
◆ 6 euro il mezzo chilo. Ne vuole?
- No, basta così, grazie.
1 kg apples; 250 g mushrooms; half kg tomatoes

5 - Vorrei mezzo chilo di questi **pomodori**.
◆ Prendo **queste** banane.
- Mi dà **due chili** di patate.
◆ Una di queste **pesche**, per favore.

6 panini, formaggio, prosciutto, due bottiglie di vino, acqua minerale, frutta e verdura, olio di oliva, **mezzo chilo di caffè** … e basta.
half a kilo of coffee

7 Mi dà … mezzo chilo di queste mele; tre pesche; un litro di acqua minerale; una bottiglia di vino rosso.

Page 64

1 *a* I'd like; *b* Could you give me? *c* That's all; *d* How much is it? *e* Do you have? *f* Anything else? *g* How much are they?

2 **pizza**: pomodori, funghi, formaggio, sale, pepe, olio di oliva, farina
macedonia: fragole, arance, zucchero, pesche, banane, mele, limone
patate (potatoes) left over

3 panini; formaggio, prosciutto; pomodori; banane; mele; due bottiglie di vino; una bottiglia di acqua minerale

4 € 18,00; € 14,25; € 10,75
change € 7,00

Page 65

1 - Buongiorno. Dica.
◆ **Un chilo di mele e mezzo chilo di banane.**
- Altro?
◆ **Mezzo chilo di pomodori.**
- Basta?
◆ **Sì, basta così, grazie.**

2 - Mi dà quattro panini.
◆ E poi?
- **Vorrei una bottiglia di vino rosso e un litro di acqua minerale gassata.**
◆ Altro?
- **Un etto di prosciutto.**
◆ Quale?
- **Questo qui.**
◆ Basta così?
- **Basta così, grazie.**

3 - Buongiorno. Dica.
◆ **Quanto costa un francobollo per la Gran Bretagna?**
- Quarantuno centesimi.
◆ **Prendo due cartoline e due francobolli.**
- Altro?
◆ **Quanto costano i biglietti per l'autobus?**
- Cinquantuno.
◆ **Vorrei sei biglietti e una carta telefonica.**

Page 66

1 costano, costano, costa; 2 555; 3 10; 4 tobacconist's; 5 un giornale italiano; 6 un francobollo per l'Australia; 7 questi; 8 mezzo; 9 venticinque euro e cinquanta, settantasei euro e novantacinque; 10 € 82,15

Punto di controllo 2
Pages 67–70

1

a - Scusi signora, c'è una banca qui vicino?
◆ Sempre dritto fino al semaforo poi

giri a sinistra …
- Può parlare lentamente? Non sono italiano.
- Allora – sempre dritto, poi al semaforo giri a sinistra e in viale Torricelli c'è la Banca Popolare, a destra.

b
- Scusi, dov'è la stazione?
- Mi dispiace, non lo so – non sono di qui.
- Scusi, dov'è la stazione?
- Giri a destra al semaforo, poi prenda la prima a sinistra, cioè via Quattro Novembre, continui sempre dritto e la stazione è in fondo.
- È lontano?
- No, no – cinquecento metri.

c
- C'è una farmacia qui?
- Ce n'è una in via Cavour: sempre dritto, la prima a sinistra, poi la prima a destra. C'è una farmacia a destra fra la banca e l'ufficio postale.

a bank E; b station A; c chemist C

2 a C'è un **bar** e c'è un'**edicola** in piazza Italia.
  b **L'azienda di turismo** è a sinistra del mercato.
  c La **farmacia** è fra la banca e l'ufficio postale.

3 Roma **613 km**; Firenze **325 km**; Napoli **831 km**; Bari **915 km**

4 Il prosciutto di Parma costa € **3,50**.
  L'olio di oliva costa € **8,95**.
  Le olive costano € **2,20**.
  I pomodori costano € **0,99**.
  Il pane costa € **1,00**.
  Il formaggio costa € **3,79**.

5 a edicola; b mercato; c farmacia; d tabaccheria; e ufficio turistico; f caffè

6 a domenica; b cerotti; c villa; d patata

7 a Può parlare lentamente?; b Non sono di qui; c Non lo so; d Come si

dice in italiano?; e Può ripetere per favore?; f Mi dispiace.

8 formaggio/pizza; euro/banca; piscina/acqua; ristorante/trattoria; francobollo/cartolina; appartamento/casa; edicola/giornale; professione/lavoro

9 a **questi** funghi; b **questa** cartolina? c **questo** vino; d **queste** pesche; e **questo** ristorante; f **queste** fragole.

10 a falso; b falso; c vero; d falso; e vero; f vero; g falso

Unit 8

Page 72

2
- Buona sera, signora. Mi chiamo Enzo Pittara. Ho prenotato una camera.
- Buona sera, signore. Allora … **una camera singola, con bagno**. Sì. **Camera numero 256 – secondo piano.** Ecco la chiave.
- Grazie.

- Buona sera. Sono Stella Rossini.
- Ah … **camera doppia – matrimoniale – con bagno**?
- Sì, esatto.
- **Camera numero 124 al primo piano**, signora.
- C'è l'ascensore?
- Ecco – in fondo a destra. Il suo passaporto per favore.

- Buona sera, signora. Ho prenotato una camera – una camera doppia.
- Il suo nome?
- Barucci.
- Ah signor Barucci – **una camera a due letti al pianterreno**. Ecco la chiave – **camera numero 65**.
  sig. Pittara – single, bath, room 256, 2nd floor; sig.ra Rossini – double bed, bath, room 124, 1st floor; sig. Barucci – twin beds, room 65, ground floor.

3 **In fondo a destra** (*at the end on the right*)

Page 73

2/4

- ● Buona sera.
- ◆ Buona sera. Avete una camera per stasera?
- ● Singola o doppia?
- ◆ Singola, con bagno.
- ● **Solo per stasera?**
- ◆ Sì.

- ● Va bene – camera singola con bagno per una notte. Il suo nome?
- ◆ Bagli.
- ● Come si scrive?
- ◆ **BAGLI.**

- ● Buona sera. Vorrei una camera doppia per tre notti.
- ◆ Tre notti … allora, fino a venerdì. Un attimo, signore … Sì, va bene. Il suo nome?
- ● Theaker.
- ◆ Come si scrive?
- ● **THEAKER.**
  for three nights

3 Alberto **CENCI.**

6 Vorrei una camera …
  … singola con doccia per stasera.
  … doppia con bagno per tre notti.
  … a due letti per una settimana.
  … singola senza bagno fino a domenica.

Page 74

2

a ● Pronto. Hotel San Marco. Buongiorno.
  ◆ Buongiorno. Vorrei prenotare una camera.
  ● Sì, per quando?
  ◆ Per sabato il **12 luglio.**
  ● Un attimo … Mi dispiace, siamo al completo.
  ◆ Grazie, buongiorno.

b ● Pronto. Hotel San Marco.
  ◆ Buongiorno. Vorrei prenotare una camera singola con bagno.

- ● Per quando?
- ◆ Il 14 settembre.
- ● Per una notte?
- ◆ No, per due notti – **il 14 e il 15 settembre.**
- ● D'accordo. Un attimo.

c ● Pronto. Buongiorno. Vorrei prenotare una camera.
  ◆ Sì – per quando?
  ● Per una settimana in aprile – **dal 13 al 20 aprile.**
  ◆ Una camera singola o doppia?
  ● Doppia … con bagno.
  ◆ A due letti o matrimoniale?
  ● Matrimoniale …

a 12 July; b 14–15 September;
c 13–20 April

Page 75

2 ● Buongiorno, signora. Posso **lasciare la valigia qui?**
  ◆ Certo, **signor Belloni.** S'accomodi.

- ● Signora, sono **Luigi Ciani.** Vorrei telefonare a New York. **Posso telefonare da qui?**
- ◆ Sì, signore. Il telefono è lì sulla destra.
- ● E **posso pagare con la carta di credito**?
- ◆ Sì, sì.

- ● Scusi, **posso parlare con il direttore**?
- ◆ Il suo nome?
- ● **Lorna Tonino.**
- ◆ Un attimo, signora Tonino.

- ● Buongiorno, signora. Vorrei una camera singola per stasera.
- ◆ Con bagno? Abbiamo solo una singola senza bagno.
- ● **Posso vedere la camera?**
- ◆ Certo – un attimo … Il suo nome, per favore?
- ● **Chini.** CHINI.

sig. Belloni – leave a suitcase
L.Tonino – speak to the manager
L.Ciani – telephone/pay by credit card
sig. Chini – see the room

3 • Scusi, possiamo parcheggiare qui?
  ◆ No, mi dispiace – qui no – ma **c'è un parcheggio dietro l'albergo**. La targa della sua macchina?
  • **FI 35782.**
  behind the hotel

Page 76

1 *a* I'd like to book; *b* I've booked; *c* Have you got? *d* Can I? *e* Can we? *f* Hello

2 *a* Ho prenotato una camera singola.
  b Vorrei una camera singola con doccia.
  c Avete una camera a due letti?
  d Ha una camera matrimoniale con bagno per una notte?
  e Vorrei prenotare una camera matrimoniale per il 21 marzo.
  f Posso telefonare?

3 *a* Sì; *b* Sì; *c* Sì; *d* No; *e* No

Page 77

1 • Buongiorno, signora. Mi dica.
  ◆ **Avete una camera?**
  • Singola o doppia?
  ◆ **Singola, con bagno.**
  • Per quante notti?
  ◆ **Per stasera.**
  • Va bene, signora – camera numero 245 al secondo piano.
  ◆ **Posso vedere la camera?**
  • Certo, signora.

2 • **Buongiorno, signora, ho prenotato una camera.**
  ◆ Il suo nome, signore?
  • **Mi chiamo John Graham**
  ◆ Allora, una camera doppia con bagno.
  • **No, una camera singola con bagno.**
  ◆ … per tre notti?
  • **No, per due notti – fino al 22 agosto.**
  ◆ Che strano. Come si scrive il suo nome?

• GRAHAM
  ◆ Ah signore – sì, scusi – camera singola per due notti.
  • **Posso pagare con la carta di credito?**
  ◆ Sì, certo.

Page 78

1 camera, chiave; *2* agosto; *3* May 1st; *4* first floor; *5* breakfast; *6* car registration number; *7* posso – I, possiamo – we; *8* no; *9* albergo quattro stelle; *10* vorrei pagare con la carta di credito, vorrei telefonare

Unit 9

Page 80

2 • Scusi, c'è **un autobus per la stazione**?
  ◆ Ce n'è uno ogni mezz'ora.
  • Quando parte?
  ◆ Ce n'è uno **alle 10.00.**

  • C'è **un autobus per piazza Garibaldi**?
  ◆ **Ogni mezz'ora**, signore. Numero 25.
  • Ce n'è uno alle dieci?
  ◆ **Alle 10.00** – sì.

  • C'è **un pullman per l'aeroporto**?
  ◆ Ce n'è uno **ogni ora**.
  • Quando parte?
  ◆ Ce n'è uno **alle 11.00**, signora.
  bus to Piazza Garibaldi – every half hour, 10:00; coach to airport – every hour, 11:00.

3 C'è un pullman per l'aeroporto? C'è un autobus per la stazione? Ce n'è uno alle dieci?

Page 81

2 • A che ora parte il prossimo treno per Roma?
  ◆ **Alle 8 e 18.**
  • Grazie.

  ◆ Scusi, c'è un treno per Bologna?
  • Ce n'è **uno ogni due ore**.

- ◆ A che ora parte il prossimo?
- ● **Alle 9 e 34**.
- ◆ Grazie.

- ● A che ora parte il prossimo treno per Bergamo?
- ◆ Alle **10 e 12**.
- ● E a che ora arriva a Bergamo?
- ◆ Alle **10 e 54**.
- ● Scusi, a che ora arriva il treno da Venezia?
- ◆ Arriva alle **8 e 25**.
- ● E il treno da Padova – a che ora arriva?
- ◆ Alle **9 e 12**.
- ● Grazie.

Roma – 8.18; Bologna – 9.34; Bergamo – 10.12; Venezia – 8.25; Padova – 9.12.

3 *a* falso; *b* falso.

4 A che ora parte il prossimo treno per Firenze?; A che ora arriva a Firenze?; A che ora arriva il treno da Venezia?

Pages 82 & 83

2 ● **Bologna, andata e ritorno.** Grazie.
- ◆ Mi dà un'**andata per Milano**.
- ● Prima o seconda classe?
- ◆ **Seconda.**
- ● 35 euro
- ◆ Grazie.

- ● Due biglietti per **Verona, andata e ritorno** … e in **prima classe**. Grazie.
- ◆ **Binario 5.**

- ● Vorrei un biglietto per **Firenze, con supplemento Intercity**.
- ◆ Solo andata o andata e ritorno?
- ● Solo **andata**.

- ◆ **Roma, andata e ritorno, con supplemento rapido.** Grazie. Da che binario parte?
- ● **Binario 12.**

Bologna – return; Milano – single, second; Verona – return, first; Firenze – single, supplement; Roma – return, supplement

3 *a* Verona, Bin. 5; *b* Roma, Bin. 12.

5 ● A che ora parte il prossimo treno per Napoli?
- ◆ Alle nove e diciassette.
- ● È diretto?
- ◆ No, **deve cambiare** a Roma.

Deve cambiare? Sì

6 ● C'è un treno per Arezzo?
- ◆ Ce n'è uno alle otto e venti.
- ● Può ripetere, per favore?
- ◆ **C'è un treno che parte alle otto e venti.**
- ● Devo cambiare?
- ◆ No, **è diretto** – è l'Intercity – **deve prenotare il posto**.
- ● Non capisco.
- ◆ Il treno è l'Intercity e lei deve prenotare il posto.
- ● Quanto costa?
- ◆ € 45,70 e c'è un supplemento di € 10,60 che fanno **€ 56,30**.
- ● Scusi … non capisco …

at 8.20; he doesn't have to change; ticket costs € 56,30; he has to make a seat reservation

7 ● Dove posso comprare un biglietto per l'autobus?
- ◆ **Deve** andare in tabaccheria – ce n'è una lì, a destra.
- ● Grazie.
- ◆ Scusi, **devo** scendere qui per il Duomo?
- ● No, alla prossima fermata.
- ◆ Grazie.

Page 84

1 *a* 2; *b* 5; *c* 6; *d* 3; *e* 4; *f* 1

2 *a* alle sette; *b* alle diciannove; *c* alle undici; *d* alle ventitré; *e* alle otto e venticinque; *f* alle venti e venticinque

3 *a* Mi dà un biglietto di seconda classe; *b* C'è un autobus ogni venti minuti; *c* Deve scendere alla seconda fermata; *d* Il prossimo treno parte alle nove e venti; *e* Il biglietto costa ventidue euro.

4 *a* Devo cambiare?; *b* Devo prenotare?; *c* Devo scendere qui?

Page 85

1 ● **C'è un pullman per Perugia?**
◆ Ce n'è uno ogni due ore.
● **A che ora parte il prossimo?**
◆ Alle dieci.
● **Devo prenotare?**
◆ No, non è necessario.
● **Quanto costa il biglietto?**
◆ Andata o andata e ritorno?
● **Andata e ritorno.**
◆ Quattordici euro.

2 ● **A che ora parte il prossimo treno per Orvieto?**
◆ Orvieto … alle nove e quaranta.
● **A che ora arriva a Orvieto?**
◆ Alle dieci e quarantasette.
● **Devo cambiare?**
◆ No, è diretto.
● **Vorrei un biglietto di andata e ritorno.**
◆ Prima o seconda classe?
● **Seconda classe. Da che binario parte?**
◆ Binario numero quattro.
● **Grazie.**

3 ● **Scusi, signora, a che ora parte il prossimo autobus per il centro?**
◆ Alle otto e venticinque.
● **C'è una tabaccheria qui vicino?**
◆ Ce n'è una in via Puccini – a destra al semaforo. *(There's one in via Puccini – on the right at the lights.)*

Page 86

1 ogni; *2* Non capisco; *3* Italy's premier high-speed train, the Red Arrow; *4* you have to do something; *5* at 6 p.m; *6* return; *7* from Rome; *8* ferry, hydrofoil; *9* Dobbiamo cambiare?; *10* Vorrei andare a Firenze stasera.

Unit 10

Page 90

2 ● Buongiorno, signori.
◆ Buongiorno.
● Tavolo per **tre**?
◆ Siamo in tre, sì.
● Aperitivi?
◆ Una bottiglia di **vino bianco** della regione.
● E una **birra**.

3/4
● Allora, signori, per primo abbiamo **zuppa, minestrone, cannelloni al forno,** spaghetti al pomodoro o alla carbonara e **risotto.**
◆ Cos'è la zuppa del giorno?
● È una **zuppa di carote**.
◆ Com'è il risotto?
● Ai funghi.
◆ E come sono gli spaghetti alla carbonara?
● Sono spaghetti … fatti con uova, **prosciutto**, panna, **formaggio** e pepe.
◆ Grazie.

5 ● Com'è il risotto?
● Come sono i ravioli?

Page 91

2 ● Allora, cosa prendono per primo?
◆ **Per me** il minestrone.
● Io **prendo** il risotto ai funghi … e le tagliatelle al ragù **per** mia figlia.
◆ Da bere?
● Una bottiglia di acqua minerale e una caraffa di vino bianco.
◆ Un litro?
● No, mezzo litro.

3 ● Pronta per ordinare, signora? Cosa prende per primo?
◆ **No, niente primo**, grazie.
● Allora, per secondo?
◆ Che cosa c'è?
● Allora … abbiamo pesce, filetto di maiale e l'agnello.
◆ Com'è l'agnello?

- Arrosto – con aglio e rosmarino.
- Che cosa consiglia?
- L'agnello è buono oggi – molto buono.
- Allora prendo **l'agnello**.
- E come contorno?
- **Zucchini.**
- Agnello con zucchini … Va bene.

4
- … e da bere, signora?
- Mezzo litro di acqua minerale – **non gassata** – e una caraffa di **rosso**.
- Mezzo litro? Un quarto?
- Un **quarto**.
- Ecco, signora. Buon appetito.

5 Prendo il pesce e l'insalata.

Pages 92 & 93

2
- **Signore, per favore.**
- Dolci, signori? Abbiamo **fragole**, **gelati**, **formaggi**, **torta di mele** – una specialità della casa …
- Io vorrei assaggiare un formaggio della regione. Mi piace il formaggio.
- No … non mi piace il formaggio. Prendo la torta al cioccolato.
- Niente dolce per me.
- … formaggio e torta al cioccolato. Grazie.

3
- Ecco la torta … per lei, signora?
- No, è per me la torta.
- … e il formaggio. Questo è dolcelatte, un formaggio della regione. Le piace, signora?
- Sì, **mi piace**, mi piace molto.
- Posso assaggiare?
- Sì, certo … ti piace?
- Mm – è buono, **è buonissimo**.
- Angela?
- Grazie no, **non mi piace** il formaggio.

sig.ra 1 – likes; sig. – likes;
sig.ra 2 – doesn't like

4 Mi piace il vino bianco.
Mi piace il formaggio.

6
- Tutto bene, signori?
- Sì grazie, **è delizioso – complimenti**!

- **Che buono!**
- Le piace il formaggio, signora?
- Sì – **è buonissimo.**
- Le piacciono i formaggi italiani allora?
- **Mi piacciono** tutti i formaggi!
- E, tutto bene, signora?
- Sì, grazie, la torta al cioccolato **è deliziosa**.

7
- Torta di mele per me.
- Anche per me.
- E anche per me. Allora, **torta di mele per tutti**.
- È buona questa torta. Ti piace, Luisa?
- Mi piace molto. Mi piacciono le mele. Mi piace anche il cioccolato.

They all choose apple tart.

8 Mi piacciono le fragole.
Mi piacciono le mele.

Page 94

1 *a* of the house; *b* grilled; *c* fried; *d* in season; *e* of the day; *f* baked; *g* with tomatoes

2 *primi* – risotto, ravioli, zuppa
secondi – coniglio, vitello, agnello
contorni – patate, insalata, zucchini
dolci – gelato, sorbetto, torta

3 *a* Mi piace il prosciutto.
b Mi piacciono le tagliatelle al ragù.
c Mi piace il risotto alla marinara.
d Mi piace il vitello ai funghi.
e Mi piace la torta di mele.
f Mi piacciono le fragole.
To say you don't like them, add **non** *before* **mi**.

4 *a* ottimo; *b* buonissimi; *c* squisita; *d* buone; *e* deliziosa

Page 95

1
- Buongiorno, signori. Tavolo per due?
- **Sì, per due.**
- Ecco il menù.
- **Grazie.**

- Pronti per ordinare?

- **Sì – un risotto alla marinara e i cannelloni.**
- E per secondo?
- **Cosa consiglia?**
- Il pesce è buono oggi – molto buono.
- **Il pesce e il pollo all'aglio.**
- E come contorno?
- **Patate e zucchini.**

- Ecco … pesce … e pollo. Buon appetito.
- **Vorrei una caraffa di vino rosso.**
- Un litro?
- **Mezzo litro.**

- Tutto bene? Le piace il pesce?
- **Sì, mi piace, è buonissimo.**
- Dessert, signori?
- **Cos'è la torta della casa?**
- È una torta di pere con panna. Le piacciono le pere?
- **Mi piacciono molto ma non mi piace la panna.
  Prendo un gelato e il formaggio.**
- Va bene.

Page 96

1 Un tavolo per due; *2* garlic; *3* mi piacciono; *4* Niente dolce per me; *5* Signore, per favore! *6* agnello; *7* buonissimo; *8* maiale; *9* Posso/Possiamo assaggiare il formaggio?; *10* Buon appetito!

Controllo finale
Pages 97–100

1 *c* Scusi, c'è un bar qui vicino?

2 • **Un'acqua minerale per favore – con ghiaccio.**
   ◆ Un euro e ottantadue.
     Ecco lo scontrino.
   • **Grazie, signora.**
   a € 8,18; *b* a till receipt

3 *a* Posso telefonare da qui?
   b Dov'è la toilette?
   c L'azienda di turismo è aperta oggi?
   d Quanto costano le cartoline?

4 • Dov'è l'Hotel Arcangelo?
   ◆ L'Hotel Arcangelo? … Prenda la prima a sinistra, al primo semaforo giri a destra – via Michelangelo – e l'Arcangelo è in fondo a destra.
     First left, right at the lights, into via Michelangelo, hotel is at the end on the right.

5 *a* A che ora parte il primo treno per Roma martedì?; *b* A che ora arriva a Roma?; *c* Quanto costa un biglietto di andata?

6 *d* Ho prenotato una camera singola con doccia fino a martedì.

7 • Scusi, **come si scrive il suo nome?** Grazie … camera **134** al **primo piano. Mi dà il passaporto**, per favore.

   a How do you spell your name?
   b Could you give me your passport?
   c Room 134, first floor.

8 • Il cambio oggi per la sterlina … vediamo … € **1,66**.

9 • Viaggio molto … domani e martedì lavoro a Firenze; martedì sera vado a Milano fino a giovedì mattina. Poi altri due giorni in Germania e, finalmente, domenica, vado in Francia – a casa!

   lunedì *Firenze*; **martedì** *Firenze e Milano (sera)*; **mercoledì** *Milano*; **giovedì** *Milano/Germania*; **venerdì** *Germania*; **sabato** *Germania*; **domenica** *Francia*

10 *a* Mi chiamo Paul Durand; *b* No, sono francese; *c* Abito a Nizza in Francia; *d* È sposato?; *e* Come si chiama sua moglie?; *f* Ha figli?; *g* Quanti anni ha?; *h* Che lavoro fa?; *i* Parla inglese?; *j* Le piace lo sport?

11 240 euro; duecentoquaranta euro.

12 *a* grilled meat and fish; *b* no; *c* local; *d* home cooking

grammar

Grammar explains how a language works. When you're learning a new language it really helps to learn some basic rules, which are easier to follow if you understand these essential grammatical terms.

Nouns are the words for living beings, things, places and abstract concepts: *daughter*, *designer*, *Rachel*, *shark*, *hat*, *village*, *Sicily*, *measles*, *freedom*.

Articles are **definite**: <u>the</u> house, <u>the</u> houses, or **indefinite**: <u>a</u> house, <u>an</u> area.

Gender: in Italian every noun is either masculine (m) or feminine (f). This is its gender, and you need to know a noun's gender because words used with it, such as articles and adjectives, have corresponding m and f forms.

Singular means one; **plural** means more than one.

Personal pronouns are words that take the place of a noun to avoid repeating it, e.g. *you*, *she*, *him*, *we*, *they*, *them*.

Italian has a **formal** and an **informal** word for *you* when talking to one person: **tu** is informal, used with someone you call by their first name; **lei** is used otherwise, particularly with someone older or in a position of authority.

Adjectives are words that describe nouns and pronouns: <u>*good*</u> idea; <u>*strong*</u> <u>*red*</u> wine; <u>*my*</u> fault; she's <u>*tall*</u>; it was <u>*weird*</u>. In Italian, unlike English, they change their final vowel according to what they're describing.

Adverbs add information to verbs, adjectives, other adverbs and whole sentences: *he's acting <u>weirdly</u>; <u>very</u> good idea; <u>luckily</u> he's not here*. Unlike adjectives, Italian adverbs, many of which end in **-mente**, don't change.

Agreement: when an Italian article or adjective is used with a noun, it has to agree with, i.e. match, that noun in terms of whether it's masculine or feminine, singular or plural.

The **ending** of a word is its final letter(s). In English, a verb ending in *-ed* tells you it happened in the past. Endings are more widespread in Italian: nouns, adjectives and verbs rely on them to convey essential information.

Verbs relate to doing and being, and are easy to recognise in English because you can put *to* in front of them: *to live, to be, to speak, to explore, to play, to think, to have, to need*. This is the **infinitive** of the verb, the form you find in the dictionary. Italian infinitives are identified by their ending, which is usually **-are**, **-ere** or **-ire**.

Regular verbs follow a predictable pattern, e.g. *I work, I worked, I have worked*; whereas **irregular** verbs are not predictable, e.g. *I eat, I ate, I have eaten*, and have to be learnt separately.

G1 nouns

Every single Italian noun is either masculine (m) or feminine (f). The majority of nouns end in -**o**, -**a** or -**e** in the singular. Nearly all the ones ending in -**o** are masculine, while the majority of those ending in -**a** are feminine. Some ending in -**e** are masculine, others feminine. In the plural, you don't add -**s** as in English – you change the final vowel instead.

singular		plural
ending in -**o**		-**o** changes to -**i**
vino *wine*	m	**vini** *wines*
ending in -**a**		-**a** changes to -**e**
birra *beer*	f	**birre** *beers*
ending in -**e**		-**e** changes to -**i**
motore *engine*	m	**motori** *engines*
stazione *station*	f	**stazioni** *stations*

G2 plural spellings

Nouns ending in -**io** end in -**ii** only when the **i** of -**io** is stressed:

zio *uncle*	**zii** *uncles*
figlio *son*	**figli** *sons*
ufficio *office*	**uffici** *offices*

Most nouns ending in consonant + -**co**/-**go** and -**ca**/-**ga** add **h** before the plural vowel, which keeps the hard sound of the **c** and **g**:

parco *park*, **parchi** *parks*　　**albergo** *hotel*, **alberghi** *hotels*
banca *bank*, **banche** *banks*　　**droga** *drug*, **droghe** *drugs*

...but some masculine nouns ending in vowel + -**co**/-**go** don't add **h**:
amico *friend* **amici** *friends*.

> Just as English has irregular plurals such as *man/men*, there are Italian words that don't follow the regular rules, e.g. nouns with an accent on the final vowel such as **città** *town/city*, **caffè** *coffee*, as well as borrowed words like *bar* and **chef**, are the same in both singular and plural.
>
> And a few masculine nouns are very irregular, with the plural becoming feminine and ending in -**a**, e.g. **il braccio** *arm*, **le braccia** *arms*; **un uovo** *one egg* (m), **due uova** *two eggs* (f).

G3 articles

Articles are very different in English and Italian. There are several Italian words for *the* and *a*, depending on whether the following word is m or f, singular or plural; whether it begins with a vowel or a consonant.

	before …	*a/an*	*the* (singular)	*the* (plural)
m	consonant	**un** treno	**il** treno	**i** treni
	z, s + consonant	**uno** sportello	**lo** sportello	**gli** sportelli
	vowel	**un** aereo	**l'**aereo	**gli** aerei
f	consonant	**una** strada	**la** strada	**le** strade
	vowel	**un'**agenzia	**l'**agenzia	**le** agenzie

Because it's the initial letter that decides the article, it can be different when the article and the noun are separated:

il treno *the train*   **lo stesso treno** *the same train*
una strada *a road*   **un'altra strada** *another road*

Italian doesn't normally use the indefinite article with nouns denoting occupation or religion:

Sono medico *I'm a doctor;* **È musulmana** *She's a Muslim.*

Italian uses the definite article more than English does – most noticeably in sentences like **Non mangio la carne** *I don't eat meat* – but also before:

- countries: **l'Italia** *Italy*, **gli Stati Uniti** *USA*
- abstract nouns: **abbandonare la speranza** *to give up hope*
- illnesses: **Ha la bronchite.** *He/She has bronchitis.*

The combines with: **a** *at/to*; **da** *from*; **di** *of*; **in** *in*; **su** *on.*

	il	**lo**	**l'**	**la**	**i**	**gli**	**le**
a	al	allo	all'	alla	ai	agli	alle
da	dal	dallo	dall'	dalla	dai	dagli	dalle
di	del*	dello*	dell'*	della*	dei*	degli*	delle*
in	nel	nello	nell'	nella	nei	negli	nelle
su	sul	sullo	sull'	sulla	sui	sugli	sulle

*these words can mean *some* as well as *of the*

adjectives

In Italian, an adjective agrees with what it describes according to whether that is masculine or feminine, singular or plural. This does not mean that they always end in the same vowel.

Adjectives ending in **-o** in the dictionary have four possible endings:		
	singular	plural
m	vino italian**o** motore italian**o**	vini italian**i** motori italian**i**
f	birra italian**a** stazione italian**a**	birre italian**e** stazioni italian**e**
Adjectives ending in **-e** have only two possible endings:		
m	vino frances**e** motore frances**e**	vini frances**i** motori frances**i**
f	birra frances**e** stazione frances**e**	birre frances**i** stazioni frances**i**

An Italian adjective generally goes after its noun when the two are together, e.g. **la musica classica, un evento speciale**. Sometimes, though, an adjective is put before the noun to give it emphasis: **uno speciale evento** *a (truly) special event*.

Colours and nationalities always go after the noun: **la Casa Bianca** *the White House*, **fagioli neri** *black beans*, **chitarra spagnola** *Spanish guitar*.

Numbers go before the noun: **prima divisione** *first division*, **seconda classe** *second class*; and a few widely used adjectives go before the noun too, although they can also go after it for emphasis, e.g.

bello *beautiful*	**bravo** *good/clever*	**buono** *good*
caro *dear (person)*	**brutto** *ugly*	**cattivo** *bad*
nuovo *new*	**giovane** *young*	**vecchio** *old*
stesso *same*	**grande** *big*	**piccolo** *small*
lungo *long*	**vero** *real*	

Molto *a lot of* belongs on this list too: **molto vino** *a lot of wine*, **molta birra** *a lot of beer*. This is different from the adverb **molto** *very* which doesn't change.

> Because of the different position of adjectives, Italian abbreviations can be the opposite of their English counterparts, e.g. the Italian for the *EU* is **UE (Unione Europea).**

G5 verbs

There are three main groups of Italian verbs, their infinitives ending in -**are**, -**ere** and -**ire**, e.g. **abitare** *to live*, **vendere** *to sell*, **partire** *to leave*. Removing the infinitive ending leaves you with the verb stem: **abit-**, **vend-**, **part-**. Other endings can then be added to the stem to convey specific information: **abito** *I live*, **vende** *s/he sells*, **partono** *they leave*. Each of the three verb groups has sets of endings, which can be used for all regular verbs in that group.

G6 regular verbs: present tense

This set of endings indicates that the verb is happening at the present time, conveying the English *I live*, *I'm living* and *I do live*. The -**ire** group follows one of two patterns, one of them inserting -**isc** in some parts.

	abit**are** *to live*	vend**ere** *to sell*	part**ire** *to leave*	cap**ire** *to understand*
io *I*	abit**o** *I live*	vend**o** *I sell*	part**o** *I leave*	cap**isco** *I understand*
tu *you*	abit**i**	vend**i**	part**i**	cap**isci**
lei, lui/lei *you, he/she it*	abit**a**	vend**e**	part**e**	cap**isce**
noi *we*	abit**iamo**	vend**iamo**	part**iamo**	cap**iamo**
voi *you*	abit**ate**	vend**ete**	part**ite**	cap**ite**
loro *they*	abit**ano**	vend**ono**	part**ono**	cap**iscono**

Verbs are always set out in this order, with or without the words for *I, you, s/he, we, they*. These tend to be included only for emphasis, contrast or clarification because the ending of the verb is generally enough to show who's doing something.

The **lui/lei** verb ending is also the one used to say '*it*' does something. The word *it* is not translated into Italian.

There are three words for *you*, and the verb has a different ending depending on which one you're using:
   tu: someone you call by their first name
   lei: someone you don't know well, older or in a position of authority
   voi: more than one person

Other common verbs that are regular in the present tense include the following. Verbs ending in -**are** are by far the most common, with only a handful of them irregular.

-are	-ere	-ire
aiutare *to help*	**chiedere** *to ask*	**aprire*** *to open*
aspettare *to wait for*	**credere** *to believe*	**costruire** *to build*
cercare *to look for*	**discutere** *to discuss*	**dormire*** *to sleep*
comprare *to buy*	**leggere** *to read*	**finire** *to finish*
dimenticare *to forget*	**mettere** *to put*	**preferire** *to prefer*
giocare *to play*	**perdere** *to lose*	**pulire** *to clean*
guidare *to drive*	**prendere** *to take/have*	**seguire*** *to follow*
invitare *to invite*	**ripetere** *to repeat*	**sentire*** *to hear*
nuotare *to swim*	**rispondere** *to answer*	**scoprire****to discover*
sognare *to dream*	**scrivere** *to write*	***no -isc**

gioco *I play*
credi *you believe*
lui risponde *he's answering*
aspettiamo *we're waiting*
cercate *you're looking for*
aiutano *they help*

G7 **asking questions**

Italian questions don't use extra words like *do* or *does*. You raise the pitch of your voice at the end so that it sounds like a question.

Angelo parte oggi. *Angelo leaves/is leaving today.*
Angelo parte oggi? *Is Angelo leaving today?*
Arriva in ritardo. *It's arriving late.*
Arriva in ritardo? *Is it arriving late?*
Capiscono. *They understand.*
Capiscono? *Do they understand?*

G8 **negatives**

Do and *does* are not used in negatives either. To say something negative, you simply put **non** in front of the verb.

Lavoro a Roma. *I work/I'm working in Rome.*
Non lavoro a Roma. *I don't work/I'm not working in Rome.*
Non capiscono. *They don't understand.*
Non capiscono? *Don't they understand?*

G9 key irregular verbs

Some of the most commonly used verbs are irregular, i.e. they don't follow the regular patterns and have to be learnt separately.

	essere *to be*		stare *to be (talking about health)*	
io	**sono**	*I am*	**sto**	*I am*
tu	**sei**	*you are*	**stai**	*you are*
lei lui/lei	**è**	*you are* *he/she is* *it is*	**sta**	*you are* *he/she is* *it is*
noi	**siamo**	*we are*	**stiamo**	*we are*
voi	**siete**	*you are*	**state**	*you are*
loro	**sono**	*they are*	**stanno**	*they are*

	avere *to have*		fare *to do/make*	
io	**ho**	*I have*	**faccio**	*I do*
tu	**hai**	*you have*	**fai**	*you do*
lei lui/lei	**ha**	*you have* *he/she has* *it has*	**fa**	*you do* *he/she does* *it does*
noi	**abbiamo**	*we have*	**facciamo**	*we do*
voi	**avete**	*you have*	**fate**	*you do*
loro	**hanno**	*they have*	**fanno**	*they do*

	andare *to go*		venire *to come*	
io	**vado**	*I go*	**vengo**	*I come*
tu	**vai**	*you go*	**vieni**	*you come*
lei lui/lei	**va**	*you go* *he/she goes* *it goes*	**viene**	*you come* *he/she comes* *it comes*
noi	**andiamo**	*we go*	**veniamo**	*we come*
voi	**andate**	*you go*	**venite**	*you come*
loro	**vanno**	*they go*	**vengono**	*they come*

	dare *to give*		**dire** *to say*	
io	**do**	*I give*	**dico**	*I say*
tu	**dai**	*you give*	**dici**	*you say*
lei lui/lei	**dà***	*you give he/she gives it gives*	**dice**	*you say he/she says it says*
noi	**diamo**	*we give*	**diciamo**	*we say*
voi	**date**	*you give*	**dite**	*you say*
loro	**danno**	*they give*	**dicono**	*they say*

	potere *be able to*	**dovere** *to have to*	**volere** *to want*
io	**posso** *I can/am able to*	**devo** *I have to/must*	**voglio** *I want*
tu	**puoi** *you can*	**devi** *you must*	**vuoi** *you want*
lei lui/lei	**può** *you can* *he/she can* *it can*	**deve** *you must* *he/she must* *it must*	**vuole** *you want* *he/she wants* *it wants*
noi	**possiamo** *we can*	**dobbiamo** *we must*	**vogliamo** *we want*
voi	**potete** *you can*	**dovete** *you must*	**volete** *you want*
loro	**possono** *they can*	**devono** *they must*	**vogliono** *they want*

Potere, **dovere** and **volere** are known grammatically as **modal verbs**. The verb following them is in the infinitive:

Posso vedere? *May I see? Can I see?*
Puoi aspettare se vuoi. *You can wait if you want.*
Dovete mostrare i passaporti. *You have to show passports.*
Marta vuole sapere. *Marta wants to know.*

Vorrei *I would like to* also comes from **volere**, but not from the present tense: **Vorrei sapere**. *I'd like to know.*

*There are two written accents in Italian: ´ and `. They indicate a final stressed vowel: **città**, **caffè**, **ragù**, **perché**, or distinguish between two words which otherwise look and sound the same: **da** *from*, **dà** *give/s*.

wordpower

You can dramatically increase your Italian by knowing which English and Italian words have shared ancestors and how they relate to each other. The spelling of some might not be identical but the meaning becomes clear when you say them. Others look similar written down but sound different as they have the stress in a different part of the word (underlined below).

nouns

Here are some of the endings to look out for:

🇬🇧	🇮🇹	
ism	ismo	altru<u>i</u>smo, razz<u>i</u>smo, sess<u>i</u>smo
ist	ista	femmin<u>i</u>sta, sciovin<u>i</u>sta, tur<u>i</u>sta
nce	nza	dist<u>a</u>nza, influ<u>e</u>nza, pazi<u>e</u>nza
nt	nte/nto	deterg<u>e</u>nte, elef<u>a</u>nte, resid<u>e</u>nte, docum<u>e</u>nto
ologist	ologo	cardi<u>o</u>logo, ec<u>o</u>logo, psic<u>o</u>logo
or/our	ore	dott<u>o</u>re, od<u>o</u>re, profess<u>o</u>re
sion	sione	impressi<u>o</u>ne, occasi<u>o</u>ne, passi<u>o</u>ne
tion	zione	conversazi<u>o</u>ne, emozi<u>o</u>ne, promozi<u>o</u>ne
ction	zione	azi<u>o</u>ne, introduzi<u>o</u>ne, reazi<u>o</u>ne
ty	tà	difficolt<u>à</u>, opportunit<u>à</u>, umanit<u>à</u>
y	ia	batter<u>i</u>a, autonom<u>i</u>a, tecnolog<u>i</u>a, ind<u>u</u>stria

Many English nouns are used routinely in Italian, e.g. **weekend, shopping, sport, stress** plus many words relating to technology, e.g. **computer, tablet, internet, software, password, mouse, hashtag, wifi.** Watch out though for pronunciation, which might not be as you're used to.

Not all Italian nouns mean what they appear to mean: **camera** means *room, camera* is **macchina fotografica**; **cantina** means *cellar, canteen* is **mensa**; **magazzino** means *warehouse, magazine* is **rivista**; **mobile** means *furniture, mobile phone* is **telefonino**; **ostriche** means *oysters, ostrich* is **struzzo**; **parenti** means *relatives, parents* are **genitori**; **preservativo** means *condom, preservative* is **conservante; rumore** means *noise, rumour* is **voce**; **tasto** means *(keyboard) key*, *taste* is **gusto**.

adjectives

It's possible to describe and comment simply but effectively by using **essere**, **molto** *very*, and the many adjectives that are similar in English and Italian.

🇬🇧   🇮🇹

-al   **-ale**, with the stress on **-ale**
Sei una persona speciale. *You're a special person.*
È eccezionale ... fenomenale! *It's exceptional ... phenomenal!*
La zona industriale è a nord. *The industrial park is to the north.*

-ble   **-bile**, with the stress on the vowel before **-bile**
È incredibile/inevitabile. *It's incredible/inevitable.*
Non è possibile. *It's not possible.* **È impossibile.** *It's impossible.*
Questo non è riciclabile. *This isn't recyclable.*

-ic(al)   **-ico**, with the stress on the third syllable from the end
Sono allergico al cioccolato. *I'm allergic to chocolate.*
Mia figlia è asmatica. *My daughter is asthmatic.*
Sono tipici della regione. *They're typical of the region.*

-nt   **-nte**, with the stress on **-ant/-ent**
È molto importante; è urgente! *It's very important; it's urgent!*
Siete così pazienti. *You're (all/both) so patient.*
Il rumore è intermittente. *The noise is intermittent.*

-ous   **-oso**, with the stress on **-oso**
Lei è molto generoso. *You're very generous.*
La pizza è deliziosa. *The pizza's delicious.*
È un progetto politico ambizioso. *It's an ambitious political project.*

As with nouns, not all adjectives mean what they appear to mean: **caldo** means *hot*, *cold* is **freddo**; **bravo** means *good* or *clever*, *brave* is **coraggioso**; **grosso** means *big*, *gross* is **volgare**; **morbido** means *soft*, *morbid* is **morboso**; **simpatico** means *nice* or *pleasant*, *sympathetic* is **comprensivo**; **tremendo** means *dreadful*, *tremendous* is **fantastico**.

verbs

There are a great many Italian verbs that are easy to recognise but there's an important difference in the position of the stress, which is not the same in the three groups.

-ire and -are verbs

In English verbs the stress varies from word to word: *imitate*, *abolish*, *control*, but it never moves from there. In Italian verbs ending in **-are** and **-ire**, the stress in the infinitive is always on the ending: **imitare**, **abolire**, **controllare**, but this changes with other endings.

-are verbs that are similar to their English translations include **analizzare, anticipare, arrivare, celebrare, considerare, detestare, economizzare, informare, migrare, organizzare, usare, verificare**.

-ire verbs include **convertire, definire, finire, servire, unire**.

-ere verbs

In the infinitive of **-ere** verbs, the stress is not on the ending but very often in the same place as the corresponding English verb, e.g. **corrispondere, decidere, dipendere, esistere, escludere, includere, invadere, offendere, ricevere, risolvere, spendere**.

Like English, Italian has many new verbs relating to new development, largely in the field of technology. Many of them tend to be the English version + **-are**, and they use regular **-are** endings, e.g. **cliccare, chattare, formattare, postare, twittare, taggare**. However, *to search* is **cercare**, *to save* is **salvare** and *to scan* is **scannerizzare**.

Verbs that don't mean what they appear to mean include:

accomodare *to fix*	*to accommodate* is **alloggiare**
assistere *to attend, be present*	*to assist* is **aiutare**
attendere *to wait, wait for*	
cancellare *to delete*	*to cancel* is **disdire, annullare**
confrontare *to compare*	*to confront* is **affrontare**
pretendere *to claim, expect*	*to pretend* is **fingere**
succedere *to happen*	*to succeed* is **riuscire**

Test your knowledge with our online quiz at www.bbcactivelanguages.com/ItalianGrammarQuiz

top ten essentials

1 Describing and commenting:
   È stupendo! *It's amazing, superb!*
   Non è accettabile. *It isn't acceptable.*

2 Talking about what's available:
   C'è acqua. *There's water.* **Non c'è acqua?** *Is there no water?*
   Ci sono testimoni. *There are witnesses.*

3 Talking about having:
   Ho una bici. *I've got a bike.* **Non hai soldi?** *Don't you have any money?*
   Abbiamo delle domande. *We have some questions.*

4 Asking what things are:
   Cos'è questo? *What is this?* **Cosa sono?** *What are they?*
   Come si dice in italiano ...? *How do you say ... in Italian?*

5 Asking where things are:
   Dov'è l'uscita/l'entrata? *Where is the exit/entrance?*
   Dove sono gli altri? *Where are the others?*

6 Saying what you like or dislike:
   (Non) mi piace sciare. *I (don't) like skiing.*
   (Non) mi piacciono le cozze. *I (don't) like mussels.*

7 Saying you would like (to do) something:
   Vorrei una risposta. *I'd like a reply.*
   Vorrei rispondere. *I'd like to reply.*

8 Saying/asking if you can do something:
   Posso chiedere perché? *Can I ask why?*
   Possiamo tornare domani. *We can come back tomorrow.*

9 Saying/asking if you have to do something:
   Devo spiegare? *Do I have to/Must I explain?*
   Dobbiamo partire. *We have to leave.*

10 Asking somebody to do something:
   Può ripetere per favore? *Please could you say that again?*
   Può parlare (più) lentamente? *Could you speak (more) slowly?*
   ...sto imparando l'italiano. *I'm learning Italian.*

Italian–English glossary

This glossary contains all those words and phrases, and their meanings, as they occur in **Talk Italian**. Parts of verbs are given in the form in which they occur, usually followed by the infinitive in brackets.

A

a to, at, in
a due passi very near
abbiamo (avere) we have
abitare to live
abolire to abolish
accettabile acceptable
accomodare to fix
accordo: d'accordo agreed; OK
l'acqua water
l'acqua minerale mineral water
l'adulto adult
l'aereo plane
aerobico aerobic
affrontare to confront
l'agenzia agency
l'aglio garlic
l'agnello lamb
agosto August
aiutare to help
al, all', allo, ai, agli, alla, alle at the; to the
l'albergo hotel
l'alimentari (m) grocer's shop
l'aliscafo hydrofoil
allergico allergic
alloggiare to accommodate; to stay
allora then; well
alto high
altro other
Altro? Anything else?
l'amaro bitter liqueur
ambizioso ambitious
americano American
l'amico/a (m/f) friend
analizzare to analyse
anch'io me too

anche also
andare to go
l'andata single (ticket)
l'andata e ritorno return
andiamo (andare) we go; we're going; let's go
l'anno year
anticipare to anticipate
l'antipasto starter
l'aperitivo aperitif
aperto open
l'appartamento flat; apartment
l'appetito appetite
aprile April
aprire to open
l'arancia orange
l'aranciata fizzy orange drink
archeologico archaeological
l'architetto architect
l'architettura architecture
arrivare to arrive
arrivederci goodbye
l'arrivo arrival
arrivo (arrivare) I arrive
arrosto roast
l'arte (f) art
l'artista (m/f) artist
l'ascensore (m) lift
asmatico asthmatic
aspettare to wait (for)
l'aspirina aspirin
assaggiare to taste
assistere to attend
assortito assorted
attendere to wait (for)
l'attenzione (f) attention
l'attimo moment

l'attore/attrice (m/f) actor
l'Australia Australia
australiano Australian
l'autobus bus
l'autonomia autonomy
l'autore/autrice (m/f) author
avere to have
avete (avere) you (pl) have
l'azienda di turismo tourist office
l'azione (f) action

B

il bagno bath, bathroom
il bambino child
la banana banana
la banca bank
il bar bar
il barista barman
basso low
Basta That's enough/all
la batteria battery; drums
bello beautiful
bene well: Va bene That's fine
bere to drink
bianco white
la biblioteca library
il bicchiere (drinking) glass
la bici; bicicletta bike; bicycle
il bigliettaio ticket seller
il biglietto ticket
il binario platform
la biodiversità biodiversity

la birra beer
la bistecca steak
bollito boiled
bolognese from Bologna
la bottiglia bottle
bravo good; clever
Bravo! Well done!
i broccoli broccoli
la bronchite bronchitis
brutto ugly
Buon appetito! Enjoy your meal!
buona notte good night
buona sera good evening
buongiorno hello
buonissimo very good indeed
buono good

C
c'è there is
il caffè coffee
il caffellatte milky coffee
caldo hot
cambiare to change
il cambio rate of exchange
la camera room
la Camera di Commercio Chamber of Commerce
la campagna country(side)
il campeggio campsite
il campo da tennis tennis court
il Canada Canada
canadese Canadian
cancellare to delete
la cannella cinnamon
la cantina cellar
capire to understand
capisco (capire) I understand
il cappuccino frothy coffee
il capretto goat (kid)
la caraffa carafe
il carboidrato carbohydrate
il/la cardiologo/a cardiologist

caro dear
la carota carrot
la carta di credito credit card
la carta telefonica phone card
la cartolina postcard
la casa house; home
la casalinga housewife
casareccio home-made
la cassa cash desk
la cassiera (f) cashier
il cassiere (m) cashier
catastrofico catastrophic
la categoria category
cattivo bad
ce n'è uno/a there is one (of them)
celebrare to celebrate
la cena dinner
il centesimo Italian currency
il centro centre
il centro città town centre
il centro storico old town
la ceramica ceramic
cercare to look for
il cerotto sticking-plaster
certo certainly
che which; that; who
che how: Che strano! How odd!
che cosa?; cosa? what?
che?; che cosa? what?
chiamare to call
chiamarsi to be called
la chiave key
chiedere to ask
il chilo kilo
chiuso closed
ci sono there are
Ciao! Hi! /Bye!
la ciliegia cherry
Cin cin! Cheers!
il cinema (m) cinema
il cinghiale wild boar
il cioccolato chocolate
cioè that is
la cipolla onion
la città town, city
civile civil

la classe class
cliccare to click
la coca coke
il cognome surname
la colazione; prima colazione breakfast
Com'è …? What's … like?
come how
completo full
Complimenti! Congratulations!
comprare to buy
la comunicazione communication
con with
la conclusione conclusion
confrontare to compare
il coniglio rabbit
considerare to consider
consigliare to recommend
il contorno side dish
controllare to control; to check
il controllo control; check
la conversazione conversation
convertire to convert
il coperto cover charge
coraggioso brave
corretto: caffè corretto coffee with alcohol
corrispondere to correspond
il corso course
Cos'è …? What is …?
la cosa thing
così so; like this/that
costa: Quanto costa? How much is (it)?
costruire to build
la cozza mussel
credere to believe
la cucina cooking; kitchen
la cugina (f) cousin
il cugino (m) cousin
culturale cultural

D
da from
dà (dare) give/s; Mi dà

...? Could you give me ...?
dal, dall', dallo, dai, dagli, dalla, dalle from the
la Danimarca Denmark
la danza dance
dare to give
decidere to decide
definire to define
del, dell', dello, dei, degli, della, delle of the; some
delizioso delicious
il/la dentista dentist
destra right; a/sulla destra on the right
il detergente detergent
detestare to detest
deve (dovere) you must
devo (dovere) I must
di of; from
Dica/Mi dica (dire) Can I help you?
dice (dire) say/s; Come si dice ...? How do you say ...?
dicembre December
dietro behind
la difficoltà difficulty
digitale digital
dimenticare to forget
il dipartimento department
dipendere to depend
dire to say
diretto direct
il direttore manager
discutere to discuss
disdire to cancel
disoccupato unemployed
dispiace: Mi dispiace I'm sorry
la distanza distance
diverso diverse; various
divorziato divorced
dobbiamo (dovere) we must
la doccia shower
il documento document
il dolce dessert

il dolcelatte dolcelatte cheese
il dolcificante sweetener
la domanda question
la domenica Sunday
doppio double
dormire to sleep
il/la dottore/ssa doctor
Dov'è ...? Where is ...?
dove where
dovere to have to
dritto, sempre dritto straight on
il duomo cathedral

E

e and
è (essere) he/she/it is; you are
eccellente excellent
eccezionale exceptional
ecco here is/are
l'ecologo ecologist
economizzare to economise
l'edicola newspaper kiosk
Edimburgo Edinburgh
l'elefante (m) elephant
l'emozione (f) emotion
l'entrata entrance
esatto exactly
escludere to exclude
esistere to exist
l'espresso espresso coffee
essere to be
l'età age
l'etto 100 grams
l'euro euro
l'evento event

F

fa/fai (fare) you do; Che lavoro fa/fai? What work do you do?
il fagiolo bean
falso false
la famiglia family
fare to do; to make
la farmacia chemist's shop

febbraio February
fenomenale phenomenal
la fermata (bus)stop
ferro: ai ferri barbecued; grilled
i figli sons; children
la figlia daughter
il figlio son
il filetto fillet
finale final
finalmente finally; at last
fingere to pretend
finire to finish
fino a as far as; until
fiorentino from Florence; Florentine
Firenze Florence
il/la fisioterapista physiotherapist
fondamentale fundamental
il fondo end, bottom; in fondo at the end of
il formaggio cheese
forno oven; al forno baked
la fotografia photograph; photography
fra between
la fragola strawberry
francese French
la Francia France
il francobollo stamp
i fratelli brothers (and sisters)
il fratello brother
la freccia arrow
freddo cold
fritto fried
il frullato milkshake
la frutta fruit
fumatori smoking
il fungo mushroom; ai funghi with mushrooms

G

la galleria gallery
il Galles Wales
gallese Welsh
gassata sparkling; non

gassata still
il gelato ice cream
i gemelli twins
generoso generous
il genitore parent
gennaio January
la Germania Germany
il ghiaccio ice
il giardino garden
giocare to play (game)
il giornale newspaper
il/la giornalista journalist
il giorno day
giovane young
il giovedì Thursday
girare to turn
giugno June
gli the
la Gran Bretagna Britain
grande big
la grappa spirits
il grasso fat
gratuito free
grave serious
grazie thank you
la Grecia Greece
griglia: alla griglia grilled;
barbecued
grosso big
guardare to look at
la guida guide; guidebook
guidare to drive
il gusto taste

H

ha (avere) he/she has;
you have
hai (avere) you have
ho (avere) I have
l'hotel hotel

I

i, il the
imitare to imitate
imparare to learn
l'impiegato/a (m/f) office
worker
importante important
impossibile impossible
l'impressione (f)

impression
in in, to
includere to include
incluso included
incredibile incredible
l'indirizzo address
l'industria industry
industriale industrial
inevitabile inevitable
l'infermiera nurse
informare to inform
l'informatica IT
le informazioni
information, news
l'ingegnere (m/f)
engineer
l'Inghilterra England
inglese English
l'ingrediente (m)
ingredient
l'ingresso entrance
innocente innocent
l'insalata salad
integrale whole
intermittente
intermittent
internazionale
international
l'introduzione (f)
introduction
invadere to invade
invitare to invite
io I
l'ipermercato
hypermarket
l'Irlanda Ireland
irlandese Irish
l'Israele Israel
l'Italia Italy
italiano Italian

L

la, l', le, lo the
lasciare to leave
lavorare to work
il lavoro work; job
leggere to read
lei you (formal), she
lentamente slowly
lesso boiled

il letto bed
lì there; over there
il litro litre
lo the; it
Londra London
lontano far
loro they
luglio July
lui he
il lunedì Monday
lungo long; caffè lungo
coffee with added water
il Lussemburgo
Luxembourg
il lusso luxury

M

ma but
macchiato: caffè
macchiato coffee with a
dash of milk
la macchina car
la macchina fotografica
camera
la macedonia fruit salad
la madre mother
il magazzino department
store; warehouse
maggio May
il maiale pig; pork
il manzo beef
marinara: alla marinara
with seafood
il marito husband
il martedì Tuesday
marzo March
il materiale material
matrimoniale double
bedded (room)
il medico doctor
medio middle: il Medio
Oriente the Middle East
la mela apple
il melone melon
la mensa canteen
il menù menu
il mercato market
il mercoledì Wednesday
la metro, la
metropolitana

underground
mettere to put
mezz'ora half an hour
mezzo half
migrare to migrate
mila thousands
mille one thousand
minerale mineral
la minestra soup
il minestrone thick vegetable soup
il minuto minute
mio my
misterioso mysterious
misto mixed
il mobile piece of furniture
moderno modern
la moglie wife
molti/e many
molto very; much
molto/a a lot of
morbido soft
morboso morbid
mostrare to show
il motore engine
il municipio town hall
il museo museum
musulmano Muslim

N

la nazionalità nationality
ne of it; of them
necessario necessary
il negozio shop
nel, nell', nello, nei, negli, nella, nelle in the
niente nothing, no
Nizza Nice
no no
noi we
il nome name
non not
la nonna grandmother
i nonni grandparents
il nonno grandfather
il nord north
la Norvegia Norway
la notte night

novembre November
il numero number
il numero di telefono phone number
numeroso numerous
nuotare to swim
nuovo new
i nutrienti nutrients

O

l'occasione (f) occasion
l'occupazione occupation
l'odore (m) smell
offendere to offend
offrire to offer
oggi today
ogni every
l'Olanda Holland
l'olio oil; olio di oliva olive oil
l'oliva olive
l'opportunità opportunity
l'ora hour; time
ordinare to order
organizzare to organise
l'organizzazione organisation
orribile horrible
l'ospedale (m) hospital
l'ostrica oyster
ottimo excellent
ottobre October

P

il padre father
il padrone boss; proprietor
il paese country; village
pagare to pay
il palazzo palace; block of flats
il pane bread; pane integrale wholemeal bread
il panino bread roll
la panna cream
panoramico panoramic
parcheggiare to park
il parcheggio car park
il parco park
il/la parente relative

parlare to speak; to talk
la partenza departure
particolare particular; special
partire to leave; to depart
il passaporto passport
la passione passion
il passo step
la patata potato
le patate fritte chips
paziente patient
la pazienza patience
la pensione guesthouse
pensione: in pensione retired
il pepe pepper
per for
per favore please
la pera pear
perché because
perché? why?
perdere to lose
perfetto perfect
la periferia outskirts; suburbs
la persona person
la pesca peach
il pesce fish
il petto breast
piacciono: mi piacciono I like (them)
piace: mi piace I like (it)
Piacere Pleased to meet you
il piano floor
il pianterreno ground floor
la piantina map
il piatto dish; primo piatto first course; secondo piatto main course
la piazza square
la piazzola place (in campsite)
piccolo small
i piedi feet; a piedi on foot
la pineta pine forest
la piscina swimming pool

il pisello pea
più more; plus
la pizza margherita cheese and tomato pizza
la pizzeria pizza restaurant
poi then
politico political
il pollo chicken
il pomodoro tomato
la popolazione population
il Portogallo Portugal
la posizione position
possiamo (potere) we can
possibile possible
posso (potere) I can
il posto place; seat
potere to be able to
il pranzo lunch
preferire to prefer
Prego You're welcome; Can I help?
prendere to take
prenotare to book
il preservativo condom
pretendere to claim
la prima colazione breakfast
la professionalità professionalism
la professione profession
il/la professore/ssa (m/f) teacher
il progetto project
la promozione promotion
pronto ready
Pronto Hello (on the phone)
il prosciutto ham
prossimo next
la proteina protein
lo/la psicologo/a psychologist
pulire to clean
il pullman coach
il punto di controllo checkpoint
può (potere) he/she can; you can

Q

quale? qual? which?
quando? when?
quanti? how many?
Quanto costano? How much are (they)?
quanto? how much?
questo this
la questura police headquarters
qui here

R

il/la ragioniere/a accountant
il ragù Bolognese sauce
il rapido fast train
il razzismo racism
la reazione reaction
la regione region
il/la residente resident
restare to remain
il resto change
ricevere to receive
riciclabile recyclable
riciclare to recycle
ripetere to repeat
risolvere to resolve
il risotto rice dish
rispondere to reply
la risposta reply
il ristorante restaurant
ritardo: in ritardo late
riuscire to succeed
la rivista magazine
romano Roman
il rosmarino rosemary
rosso red
il rumore noise

S

il sabato Saturday
il sale salt
Saluti Regards/Greetings
sapere to know
lo scenario scene, scenario
scendere to get down; to get off (bus/train)
sciare to ski
la scienza science

sciovinista chauvinist
lo scontrino receipt; ticket
scoprire to discover
la Scozia Scotland
scozzese Scottish
scrive: Come si scrive? How do you write it?
scrivere to write
Scusi Excuse me
secondo second
la segretaria secretary
seguire to follow
sei six
sei (essere) you are
il semaforo traffic lights
sempre always
sentire to hear; to feel
senza without
la sera evening
servire to serve
il servizio service
il sessismo sexism
settembre September
la settimana week
Sì Yes
siamo (essere) we are
la Sicilia Sicily
siciliano Sicilian
signor Mr
la signora woman; Mrs; Madam
il signore man; Sir
simpatico nice; pleasant
single unmarried
singola single
sinistra left; a/sulla sinistra on the left
la situazione situation
so (sapere) I know; non (lo) so I don't know (it)
sociale social
sognare to dream
i soldi money
solo only
sono (essere) I am; they are
il sorbetto sorbet
la sorella sister
sostenibile sustainable

la Spagna Spain
spagnolo Spanish
spazioso spacious
speciale special
la specialità speciality
specializzato specialised
spendere to spend
la speranza hope
la spiaggia beach
lo spiedo spit; allo spiedo on a spit
spiegare to explain
gli spinaci spinach
lo sportello counter
sposato married
la spremuta freshly-squeezed orange juice
squisito excellent
sta/i: Come sta/i? How are you?
la stagione season
stare to be (referring to health)
stasera this evening
gli Stati Uniti USA
la stazione station
la stella star
la sterlina pound £
stesso same
lo stile style
la storia story; history
strano strange; odd
lo struzzo ostrich
lo studente student
lo studio studio
stupendo amazing; superb
subito immediately
succedere to happen
sul, sull', sullo, sui, sugli, sulla, sulle on the
suo your; his; her
superbo superb
il supermercato supermarket
il supplemento supplement
la Svizzera Switzerland
svizzero Swiss

T

la tabaccheria tobacconist's shop
il talento talent
la targa car number plate
il tasto key (of keyboard)
il tavolo table
il tè tea
il teatro theatre
la tecnologia technology
tedesco German
telefonare to telephone
il telefonino mobile phone
il telefono telephone
terzo third
il/la testimone witness
tipico typical
il tiramisù Italian dessert
la toilette toilet
la torta cake; gateau
tradizionale traditional
la tradizione tradition
il traghetto ferry
la trattoria small family restaurant
tremendo dreadful
il treno train
trovare to find
tu you (informal)
il turismo tourism
tutti e due both
tutto all

U

l'ufficio office
l'ufficio postale post office
l'umanità humanity
umido: in umido stewed
un, un', una, uno one; a/an
unico unique
unire to unite
l'università university
l'uovo egg; le uova eggs
urgente urgent
usare to use
l'uscita exit

V

va bene that's fine; OK
la vacanza holiday; in vacanza on holiday
la valigia suitcase
vecchio old
vedere to see
vediamo (vedere) let's see
vendere to sell
il venerdì Friday
veneziano from Venice; Venetian
venire to come
verde green
la verdura vegetables
vergine virgin
verificare to verify
vero real; true
la via street
viaggiare to travel
il viale avenue
vicino near; qui vicino nearby
il vigneto vineyard
la villetta small detached house
la vitamina vitamin
il vitello veal
la voce voice; rumour
voi you (plural)
Volentieri Willingly; I'd love to/one
volere to wish; to want
volgare gross; vulgar
vorrei (volere) I'd like
vuole (volere) you want

Z

la zia aunt
lo zio uncle
la zona zone; area
lo zucchero sugar
gli zucchini courgettes
la zuppa soup

English–Italian glossary

A

a lot of molto
a/an un, un', una, uno
to abolish abolire
acceptable accettabile
to accommodate alloggiare
accountant il/la ragioniere/a
action l'azione (f)
actor l'attore/attrice (m/f)
address l'indirizzo
adult l'adulto
aerobic aerobico
age l'età
agency l'agenzia
all tutto
allergic allergico
also anche
always sempre
amazing stupendo
ambitious ambizioso
American americano
to analyse analizzare
and e
angry arrabbiato
to answer rispondere
to anticipate anticipare
Anything else? Altro?
apartment l'appartamento
aperitif l'aperitivo
appetite l'appetito
apple la mela
April aprile
archaeological archeologico
architect l'architetto
architecture l'architettura
area la zona
arrival l'arrivo
to arrive arrivare
arrow la freccia
art l'arte (f)

artist l'artista (m/f)
to ask chiedere; domandare
aspirin l'aspirina
to assist aiutare
assorted assortito
asthmatic asmatico
at the al, all', allo, ai, agli, alla, alle
to attend assistere
attention l'attenzione (f)
August agosto
aunt la zia
Australia l'Australia
Australian australiano
author l'autore/autrice (m/f)
autonomy l'autonomia
avenue il viale

B

bad cattivo
baked al forno
banana la banana
bank la banca
bar il bar
barbecued alla griglia; ai ferri
barman il barista
bath, bathroom il bagno
battery la batteria (car); la pila (small)
to be essere
to be (referring to health) stare
to be able to potere
beach la spiaggia
bean il fagiolo
beautiful bello
because perché
bed il letto
beef il manzo
beer la birra
behind dietro
to believe credere
between fra
big grande; grosso

bike; bicycle la bici; bicicletta
biodiversity la biodiversità
bit (a) un po'
block of flats il palazzo; il condominio
boar il cinghiale
boiled bollito; lesso
Bolognese bolognese; sauce il ragù
to book prenotare
boss il padrone
both tutti e due
bottle la bottiglia
brave coraggioso
bread il pane
bread roll il panino
breakfast la colazione; prima colazione
Britain la Gran Bretagna
broccoli i broccoli
bronchitis la bronchite
brother il fratello
brothers (and sisters) i fratelli
to build costruire
bus l'autobus (m)
bus stop la fermata
but ma
to buy comprare

C

cake la torta
to call chiamare
camera la macchina fotografica
campsite il campeggio
Canada il Canada
Canadian canadese
to cancel disdire
canteen la mensa
car la macchina
car number plate la targa
car park il parcheggio
carafe la caraffa
carbohydrate il

carboidrato
cardiologist il/la cardiologo/a
carrot la carota
cash desk la cassa
cashier il/la cassiere/a
cat il gatto
catastrophic catastrofico
category la categoria
cathedral il duomo; la cattedrale
to celebrate celebrare; festeggiare
cellar la cantina
cent (Italian currency) il centesimo
centre il centro
ceramic la ceramica
certainly certo; certamente
Chamber of Commerce la Camera di Commercio
change il resto
to change cambiare
chauvinist sciovinista
to check controllare
checkpoint il punto di controllo
Cheers! Cin cin! Salute!
cheese il formaggio
chemist's shop la farmacia
cherry la ciliegia
chicken il pollo: breast petto di pollo
child il bambino
children i bambini; i figli
chips le patate fritte
chocolate il cioccolato
Christian cristiano
cinema il cinema (m)
cinnamon la cannella
city la città
civil civile
to claim pretendere (to demand); affermare (to assert, to maintain)
class la classe
classic, classical classico

to clean pulire
clean pulito
clever bravo (able, skilful); intelligente (smart)
to click cliccare
closed chiuso
coach il pullman; la corriera
coffee il caffè
coffee with a dash of milk il caffè macchiato
coffee with added water il caffè americano/lungo
coffee with alcohol il caffè corretto
coffee (milky) il cappuccino; il caffellatte
coke la coca
cold freddo
to come venire
communication la comunicazione
to compare confrontare
computer il computer
conclusion la conclusione
condom il preservativo
to confront affrontare
Congratulations! Complimenti!
to consider considerare
control il controllo
to control controllare
conversation la conversazione
to convert convertire
cooking la cucina
to correspond corrispondere
counter lo sportello
country il paese
country(side) la campagna
courgette la zucchina; lo zucchino
course il corso
cousin il/la cugino/a

cover charge il coperto
cream la panna
credit card la carta di credito
cultural culturale

D

dance la danza
daughter la figlia
day il giorno
dear caro
December dicembre
to decide decidere
to define definire
to delete cancellare
delicious delizioso
Denmark la Danimarca
dentist il/la dentista
to depart partire
department il dipartimento; il reparto
department store il grande magazzino
departure la partenza
to depend dipendere
dessert il dolce; il dessert
detergent il detergente
to detest detestare
difficulty la difficoltà
digital digitale
dinner la cena
direct diretto
to discover scoprire
to discuss discutere
dish il piatto
distance la distanza
diverse diverso; vario
divorced divorziato
to do fare
doctor il/la dottore/ssa; il medico
document il documento
dog il cane
double doppio
double room camera matrimoniale
dreadful orrendo
to dream sognare
to drink bere

to drive **guidare**

E

ecologist **l'ecologo**
to economise **economizzare**
Edinburgh **Edimburgo**
egg **l'uovo**: eggs **le uova**
elephant **l'elefante (m)**
emotion **l'emozione (f)**
end **la fine**; at the end of in **fondo**
engine **il motore**
engineer **l'ingegnere (m/f)**
England **l'Inghilterra**
English **inglese**
Enjoy your meal! **Buon appetito!**
entrance **l'ingresso**; **l'entrata**
espresso coffee **il caffè (espresso)**
euro **l'euro**
evening **la sera**
event **l'evento**
every **ogni**
exactly **esattamente**
Exactly! **Esatto!**
excellent **ottimo**; **squisito**; **eccellente**
exceptional **eccezionale**
exchange rate **il cambio**
to exclude **escludere**
Excuse me **Scusi**
to exist **esistere**
exit **l'uscita**
to explain **spiegare**

F

false **falso**
family **la famiglia**
far **lontano**: as far as **fino a**
fat **grasso**; **il grasso**
father **il padre**
February **febbraio**
to feel **sentire**
ferry **il traghetto**
fillet **il filetto**

final **finale**
to find **trovare**
to finish **finire**
first course **primo piatto**
fish **il pesce**
to fix **riparare**
flat **l'appartamento**
floor **il piano**
Florence; from Florence **Firenze**; **fiorentino**
flour **la farina**
flower **il fiore**
to follow **seguire**
foot **il piede**: on foot a **piedi**
for **per**
to forget **dimenticare**
France **la Francia**
free **gratuito**
French **francese**
freshly-squeezed orange juice **la spremuta d'arancia**
Friday **il venerdì**
fried **fritto**
friend **l'amico/a (m/f)**
from **da**; **di**
from the **dal**, **dall'**, **dallo**, **dai**, **dagli**, **dalla**, **dalle**
fruit **la frutta**
fruit salad **la macedonia**
full **completo**
fundamental **fondamentale**
furniture **il mobilio**; piece of furniture **il mobile**

G

gallery **la galleria**
garden **il giardino**
garlic **l'aglio**
generous **generoso**
German **tedesco**
Germany **la Germania**
to get down; get off (bus/train) **scendere**
to get on (bus/train) **salire**
to give **dare**
glass (drinking) **il**

bicchiere
to go **andare**
goat **la capra**: kid **il capretto**
good **buono**, **bravo**
good evening **buona sera**
good night **buona notte**
goodbye **arrivederci**
grandfather **il nonno**
grandmother **la nonna**
grandparents **i nonni**
Greece **la Grecia**
green **verde**
greetings **saluti**
grilled **grigliato**; **alla griglia**
grocer's shop **l'alimentari (m)**
gross **volgare**
ground floor **il pianterreno**
guesthouse **la pensione**
guide, guidebook **la guida**

H

half **mezzo**
half an hour **mezz'ora**
ham **il prosciutto**
to happen **succedere**
happy **contento**; **felice**
to have **avere**
to have to **dovere**
he **lui**
to hear **sentire**
hello **buongiorno**
Hello (on the phone) **Pronto**
to help **aiutare**
her **suo**
here **qui**
here is/are **ecco**
Hi!/Bye! **Ciao!**
high **alto**
his **suo**
history **la storia**
holiday **la vacanza**; on holiday **in vacanza**
Holland **l'Olanda**
home **la casa**

home-made fatto in casa; casareccio
hope la speranza
horrible orribile
hospital l'ospedale (m)
hot caldo
hotel l'albergo; l'hotel (m)
hour l'ora
house la casa; la villa; la villetta
housewife la casalinga
how che; come
How many? Quanti?
How much? Quanto?
How much is it/are they? Quanto costa/no?
humanity l'umanità
husband il marito
hydrofoil l'aliscafo
hypermarket l'ipermercato

I io
ice il ghiaccio
ice cream il gelato
to imitate imitare
immediately subito
important importante
impossible impossibile
impression l'impressione (f)
in in
in the nel, nell', nello, nei, negli, nella, nelle
to include includere
included incluso
incredible incredibile
industrial industriale
industry l'industria
inevitable inevitabile
information le informazioni
ingredient l'ingrediente (m)
innocent innocente
intermittent intermittente
international internazionale
introduction l'introduzione (f)
to invite invitare
Ireland l'Irlanda
Irish irlandese
Israel l'Israele
IT l'informatica
Italian italiano
Italy l'Italia

J
January gennaio
job il lavoro
journalist il/la giornalista
July luglio
June giugno

K
key la chiave
key (of keyboard) il tasto
kilo il chilo
kitchen la cucina
to know (fact) sapere
to know (person) conoscere

L
lamb l'agnello
last ultimo; at last finalmente
late in ritardo
to learn imparare
to leave lasciare; andare via (depart); partire (depart)
left sinistra; on the left a/sulla sinistra
library la biblioteca
lift l'ascensore (m)
to like piacere
litre il litro
little piccolo (small); un po' (a little bit)
to live abitare
London Londra
long lungo
to look at guardare
to look for cercare
to lose perdere

lot (a lot of) molto
low basso
lunch il pranzo
Luxembourg il Lussemburgo
luxury il lusso

M
magazine la rivista
main course secondo piatto
to make fare
man il signore
manager il direttore
many molti/e
map la piantina; la mappa
March marzo
market il mercato
married sposato
material il materiale
May maggio
melon il melone
menu il menù
middle medio: the Middle East il Medio Oriente
to migrate migrare
milkshake il frullato
mineral minerale
mineral water l'acqua minerale
minute il minuto
mixed misto
mobile phone il telefonino; il cellulare
modern moderno
moment l'attimo; il momento
Monday il lunedì
money i soldi
morbid morboso
more, plus più
mother la madre
Mr il signor(e)
Mrs la signora
museum il museo
mushroom il fungo; with mushrooms ai funghi
music la musica
Muslim musulmano

mussel la cozza
my mio
mysterious misterioso

N

name il nome; my name
is mi chiamo
national nazionale
nationality la nazionalità
near vicino
nearby qui vicino
necessary necessario
new nuovo
news le notizie
newspaper il giornale
newspaper kiosk
l'edicola
next prossimo
Nice Nizza
nice simpatico
night la notte
no no
noise il rumore
north il nord
Norway la Norvegia
not non
nothing, no niente
November novembre
number il numero
numerous numeroso
nurse l'infermiera/e
nutrients i nutrienti

O

occasion l'occasione (f)
occupation
l'occupazione (f); il
lavoro
October ottobre
odd strano
of di
of the del, dell', dello,
dei, degli, della, delle
to offend offendere
to offer offrire
office l'ufficio
office worker
l'impiegato/a (m/f)
oil l'olio
OK d'accordo; va bene

old vecchio
old town il centro
storico
olive oil olio di oliva
on su
on the sul, sull', sullo,
sui, sugli, sulla, sulle
one un, un', una, uno
onion la cipolla
only solo
open aperto
to open aprire
opportunity
l'opportunità
orange l'arancia; fizzy
orange drink l'aranciata;
orange juice la spremuta
to order ordinare
organisation
l'organizzazione (f)
to organise organizzare
ostrich lo struzzo
other altro
our nostro
outskirts la periferia
oven il forno
oyster l'ostrica

P

palace il palazzo
panoramic panoramico
parent il genitore
to park parcheggiare
park il parco
particular particolare;
specifico
passion la passione
passport il passaporto
patience la pazienza
patient paziente
to pay pagare
pea il pisello
peach la pesca
pear la pera
pepper il pepe
perfect perfetto
person la persona
phenomenal fenomenale
phone number il numero
di telefono

photograph;
photography la
fotografia
physiotherapist il/la
fisioterapista
pig il maiale
pine forest la pineta
pizza restaurant la
pizzeria
place (in campsite) la
piazzola
place, seat il posto
plane l'aereo
plaster (sticking) il
cerotto
platform il binario
to play giocare (game);
suonare (instrument)
please per favore
pleased contento;
Pleased to meet you!
Piacere!
police la polizia; police
headquarters la questura
political politico
pool la piscina
population la
popolazione
pork il maiale
Portugal il Portogallo
position la posizione
possible possibile
post office l'ufficio
postale
postcard la cartolina
potato la patata
pound £ la sterlina
to prefer preferire
to pretend fingere
profession la professione
professionalism la
professionalità
project il progetto
promotion la
promozione
protein la proteina
psychologist lo/la
psicologo/a
to put mettere
question la domanda

R

rabbit il coniglio
racism il razzismo
rate of exchange il cambio
reaction la reazione
to read leggere
ready pronto
real vero
receipt lo scontrino
to receive ricevere
to recommend consigliare
recyclable riciclabile
to recycle riciclare
red rosso
regards saluti
region la regione
relation il/la parente
to remain rimanere; restare
to repeat ripetere
reply la risposta
to reply rispondere
resident il/la residente
to resolve risolvere
restaurant il ristorante; la trattoria
retired in pensione
return l'andata e ritorno
right destra; on the right a/sulla destra
roast arrosto
Roman romano
room la camera
rosemary il rosmarino

S

salad l'insalata
salt il sale
same stesso
Saturday il sabato
to say dire
science la scienza
Scotland la Scozia
Scottish scozzese
seafood i frutti di mare; with seafood ai frutti di mare, alla marinara
season la stagione
second secondo
secretary la segretaria
to see vedere
to sell vendere
September settembre
serious grave
to serve servire
service il servizio
sexism il sessismo
shop il negozio
to show mostrare
shower la doccia
Sicilian siciliano
Sicily la Sicilia
side dish il contorno
single singolo
single (ticket) l'andata
sister la sorella
situation la situazione
to ski sciare
to sleep dormire
slowly lentamente
small piccolo
smell l'odore; il profumo
so così
social sociale
soft morbido
some del, dell', dello, dei, degli, della, delle
son il figlio
sorbet il sorbetto
Sorry! Scusi/a: I'm sorry Mi dispiace
soup la minestra; la zuppa
spacious spazioso
Spain la Spagna
Spanish spagnolo
sparkling (drink) gassato; frizzante
to speak parlare
special speciale
specialised specializzato
speciality la specialità
to spend spendere (money); passare (time)
spinach gli spinaci
spit (cooking) lo spiedo
square la piazza
stamp il francobollo
star la stella
starter l'antipasto
station la stazione
steak la bistecca
step il passo
stewed stufato; in umido
sticking-plaster il cerotto
still (drink) naturale; non gassato
story la storia
straight on dritto; sempre dritto
strange strano
strawberry la fragola
street la strada; la via
student lo/la studente/ssa
studio lo studio
style lo stile
suburbs la periferia
to succeed riuscire
sugar lo zucchero
suitcase la valigia
Sunday la domenica
superb superbo; eccezionale
supermarket il supermercato
surname il cognome
sustainable sostenibile
sweetener il dolcificante
to swim nuotare
swimming pool la piscina
Swiss svizzero
Switzerland la Svizzera

T

table il tavolo
tablet (IT) il tablet
tablet (med.) la compressa
to take prendere
talent il talento
to talk parlare
to taste assaggiare
taste il gusto
tea il tè
teacher l'insegnante

(m/f); il/la professore/ssa
technology la tecnologia
telephone il telefono
to telephone telefonare
tennis court il campo da tennis
thank you grazie
that is cioè
That's enough/all Basta
the il, l', lo, i, gli, la, le
theatre il teatro
then (after) poi; dopo
there (over there) lì
there are ci sono
there is c'è
they loro
thing la cosa
third terzo
this questo
this evening stasera
thousand mille; thousands mila
Thursday il giovedì
ticket il biglietto
ticket seller il bigliettaio
time l'ora; il tempo
to a, in
to the al, all', allo, ai, agli, alla, alle
tobacconist's la tabaccheria
today oggi
toilet la toilette
tomato il pomodoro
too anche; me too anch'io
tourism il turismo
tourist office l'azienda di turismo; l'ufficio turistico
town la città
town centre il centro città
town hall il municipio
tradition la tradizione
traditional tradizionale
traffic lights il semaforo
train il treno

to travel viaggiare
tremendous fantastico
true vero
Tuesday il martedì
to turn girare
twins i gemelli
typical tipico

U

ugly brutto
uncle lo zio
underground (trains) la metro, la metropolitana
to understand capire
unemployed disoccupato
unique unico
to unite unire
university l'università
unmarried single
until fino a
urgent urgente
USA gli Stati Uniti
to use usare

V

various diverso; vario
veal il vitello
vegetables la verdura
Venetian (from Venice) veneziano
to verify verificare
very molto
very good ottimo; buonissimo; eccellente
village il paese; il borgo; il villaggio
vineyard il vigneto
virgin vergine
vitamin la vitamina
voice la voce

W

to wait for aspettare
Wales il Galles
to want volere
warehouse il magazzino
water l'acqua
we noi
Wednesday il mercoledì
week la settimana

welcome benvenuto; you're welcome prego
well bene
Well done! Bravo!
Well then ... Allora ...
Welsh gallese
what? che?; che cosa?
when quando
where is: Where is ...? Dov'è ...?
which che
which? quale? qual?
white bianco
who che
who? chi?
whole intero, integrale
wholemeal bread pane integrale
why? perché?
wife la moglie
wild selvatico
wild boar il cinghiale
Willingly! With pleasure! Volentieri!
to wish volere; desiderare
with con
without senza
witness il/la testimone
woman la donna; la signora
to work lavorare
work (job) il lavoro
to write scrivere

Y

year l'anno
Yes Sì
you (formal) lei
you (informal) tu
you (plural) voi
young giovane
your suo; tuo; vostro

Z

zone la zona